Finding My Soul: Five Years at the Findhorn Community

FINDING MY SOUL

Five Years at the Findhorn Community

a memoir by Bonnie B Blue, MA

Sweet Lorraine Publishing
Sacramento, CA

I join hands with all the people and other living beings who have helped make this planet a beautiful and loving space to grow in. I dedicate this book to you.

As well, I dedicate this book to Maya, whose values give me hope for our future.

Contents

Introduction

"The Unexamined Life is Not Worth Living"
(quote attributed to Socrates)

This is a memoir of my journey: before, during and after my time at the spiritual community of Findhorn in Scotland. At the age of thirty-three I left my home, unhappy and looking for help. Although the community played a large part in my healing and transformation, this book is more of a personal journal covering the joys and challenges I faced and the lessons learned while a member there.

Always fascinated by the process of personal growth and transformation, I wondered, is there a pattern to it? On the surface, my story is similar to many others who traveled that path. After a difficult and at times painful earlier life, I dived deep into cleansing waters, and emerged anew. What happened in those waters is most of my book. Negativities within were faced, powerful emotions tolerated. And my relationship with God evolved into a relationship with my soul.

Learning from life's experiences is how this Earth school

functions, so I include reflections at the end of each chapter and suggestions from my work as a psychotherapist.

Although I consider myself profoundly normal, my experiences have magical tones, which is not surprising. For within every one of us is our divinely gifted soul. The more we open our heart and heal our wounds, the more our soul can step in to guide us. Bringing our whole selves forth is perhaps one of the most exciting adventures we can go on.

A second presence weaving through the book is the Findhorn Community. The place has seen thousands of visitors and many hundreds of longer-term members, all contributing to its ongoing creation. Each have their own story to tell. Mine is only one, during a particular time period, the late eighties. All this is to say, my story is uniquely mine and does not represent the experience of every member. Hopefully, the charm and flavor of the place will come through my personal lens.

Findhorn has been called magical. And the community does have a special feel to it. So many beings have infused conscious, loving intent into the soil and the stones of the place. So many hearts have opened; so many paths have crossed. The veil between the material and the spiritual, between nature and mankind, seems thinner there. It is a rarity and its essence persists, begun sixty years ago and continuing to this day.

1

As to Why? ...My Beginnings

Questions

I didn't know *why*. When asked, nothing came up. Some bubbly, happy reasons formed in my mind: being at Findhorn was an adventure, a place of growth, a way to joy, a rebirthing process. But where did the push come from? The *why* lingered in a shadowy corner of my past, and only after completing my tale did I look into that corner.

Thoughts of writing about my time at Findhorn started ten years ago. I used my office to see clients during the day. But one night a month our group met. Nanci had arrived early, and found it a perfect opportunity to ask, "What was it like, being at the Findhorn Community?" She leaned in, her grey curls framing a slight smile that seemed to anticipate my answer.

The question hung in the empty air between us.

What could I say? A thousand experiences flooded my mind. Five years at a spiritual community condensed into five minutes? Impossible. I wavered, trying to find the right words.

Nanci and I belonged to a women's spiritual group. All in our sixties, each of us brought perspectives gained from years of having our edges rubbed by life's challenges. Our friendship required a more nuanced response than "it was great" or "I loved it". My time at Findhorn was complicated: ecstatic pleasures and deep pains; understandings that shook my stability, and also built my future.

It was then I decided. "Nanci, I am going to write about it. But for now, just know it was incredible."

She did not ask, "Why Findhorn?" The place was well-known in New Age circles. We were all seekers. But while they were marrying and establishing careers in their early thirties, I left on a walk-about, intending to visit spiritual groups around the globe and hoping to find my home. My first stop was a community in a little Scottish fishing village called Findhorn. I stayed five years.

She didn't ask why I went, but others did. I could not come up with a quick answer. A great loss? A relationship breakup? A dire medical condition? Nothing quite so overt pushed me to look for something more. It was many steps along the way that led me there. Upon looking back into my family history, the answer to that puzzling question began to take shape.

Living in community came easy to me. I had always lived with others, my family being the first. My father built our home, situated in a suburb of Chicago. It was a beautiful neighborhood, with spacious yards and plenty of wild areas. My father loved growing things and tended his vegetable garden in our backyard, softly whistling under his breath as he worked. He often rushed into the kitchen excited about a large tomato or an ear of corn.

"Bonnie Beau, look at this beauty!" My eyes fixed on his shining face, tracing his happiness in my memory.

A groomed backyard was not my idea of nature. A small patch of woods behind our house caught my imagination and held my six-year-old explorer self in it's magical world. Further afield a swampland lay, complete with a broken down raft. The swamp spooked me at first. But the next year I climbed around the logs and balanced on the raft stuck in the muck. My shadow on the water caused polliwogs to skitter here and there.

When ten, my safe and happy life shook loose. My parents separated, and then divorced. Too young to understand, I now see what a mismatch they were.

My father was the thirteenth of fourteen children from a poor sharecropper family. His ancestors immigrated from Scotland and made their way across the United States to Texas. He walked to school barefoot til he could earn money for a pair of shoes. After fighting in the second world war, he joined a minor league baseball team. It became his opportunity to leave Texas and make his way to the bustling city of Chicago, where he could find a good paying job.

My mother came from new money. My grandfather started with honey. His ancestors were beekeepers to the royal families in Germany, and he carried on this tradition as a teen in Chicago. Eventually his business grew so large he hauled railcars full of honey from the west. His next venture was a restaurant. Eventually he built a motor lodge and bar. By the time he sold the property, he was worth millions.

The marriage might have looked favorable early on. But my parents' values veered off in different directions. Making money, and the pleasures it bought, drove my father. He worked long days, managing my grandfather's businesses. He relaxed by playing golf regularly at the course near his work or drinking too much with the ladies at the bar. And he loved active sports. One day my dad came home with a boat, and for a few years we spent our vacations water skiing. A natural athlete, his skills improved, until he had mastered a single ski and then dropped that to skim along the fast moving surface with his bare feet.

In many ways he was a man of his times. In the late 50's and early 60's, cocktail parties at sleek modern homes were the going rage. Our white mantle, that once held Christmas stockings, was replaced by flat grey panelling. Our Spruce Christmas trees, colorful with paper rings, popcorn vines and a variety of hanging ornaments, were exchanged for white flocked trees with turquoise balls. Eventually we unpacked a pretend tree, placing each branch into position.

Having come from money, my mother cared less about it. She yearned for children, little beings she could pour her love into. She learned to cook and created a home for us. She filled her time with crafts, and donated her creations to the Christmas bazaars our church put on. Over the years she gained weight, becoming more of a nurturing mother than a svelte wife.

The divorce rocked our world. It rocked my mother's relationship with my grandfather, who adored my father. It rocked my family's relationship with our church, where divorces were forbidden. But most importantly, it rocked my brother Billy, who was twelve. As the eldest child, my father's absence devastated him.

One day Billy pulled my younger sister, Bu, and I into his room for a meeting.

"How're you guys doing with all this?"

My heart was breaking. When I first heard of their divorce, I raced to the woods in tears, my stomach gut-punched.

"I hate it!" I said. "Billy, mom scratched dad last night! I saw him in the bathroom putting on a bandaid."

"That's why I called you in here, cause it's important that we talk about this. It's up to us now. We can't rely on mom and dad anymore. We have to be there for each other."

I loved our secret club, the vow we agreed to, feeling as though we were empowered enough to control our crashing world. Billy needed that control the most. When my mother left for work, he became the 'man of the house'.

"I want you guys to clean up. Bu, pick up your toys. Bonnie, do the dishes."

"No!" I planted my feet. "Mom never said you could tell us what to do."

"You do it or I'll make you!" He pulled out his belt.

I took off running and hid in the far corner of my closet. He tried to pull me out but I rolled into a ball as he whipped my back and shoulders. After a few horrible afternoons, I pleaded with mom not to go to work.

"Mom, Billy beats us!"

"I'm sorry, I have work. I can't do anything about that right now."

One evening, he tried to stop my mother leaving the house on a date. "You're not going out wearing those." He pointed to her black patterned nylons. "You look like a whore."

During our family turmoil, Billy stole money from my mom to buy himself a car. That action was enough to get him sent to live with my father. At sixteen, he dropped out of high school

7

and hitchhiked to California. He eventually joined the Marines. Serving a tour of duty in Vietnam, he learned to discipline his anger and channel his power, under the authority of the military. He stayed in the military for the rest of his career, becoming a legionnaire in the French Foreign Legion.

My love for him never faltered. His reaction to the separation by taking control through force was the only way he knew how. But our little three-person club dissolved quickly under those pressures.

My father married the woman who drew him out of our family. Because of shared custody, we spent our weekends at their home. I liked Joanne. She was stylish and taught me about hair and fashion. However, she made mistakes in trying to parent us.

For their first Easter she bought my sister and I matching outfits, made from a hideous blue plaid. Joanne managed to get a photo of Billy, Bu and myself dressed up just as we were leaving for church.

Shortly after, my sister nudged my brother. "Push me," she whispered.

He lightly touched her and she 'fell' into the swimming pool next to us, ruining any chance of showing up for Easter service dressed like that. The twinsy look was not for her.

Our antics and outspokenness stretched the limits of their marriage, according to my father. It did not last long. I was sorry for that, sorry for my father.

My mother used her divorce settlement to buy a blues club in Chicago's Old Town. Shortly after I graduated from grade school, we packed up our car and said goodbye to our life in the suburbs. Through the back window, my beloved neighborhood retreated into the distance.

It was the three of us, my mother, Bu and I. That would not last long. My mother built family where ever she went. Her nurturing spirit earned her the name 'Mother Blue', which also was the name of her club. When she found a stray human who needed a family, she welcomed them. Occasionally, grumbling under my breath, I crawled in with my sister so someone could have my bed. When a band came through Chicago and needed a place to crash, I found myself stepping carefully over rows of sleeping bags in our living room. The community of friends we developed centered around my mother, her infamous meals, cozy home and warm heart.

My dad resented my mom's choices. "She spent all that money, the money I made, to buy a nightclub? She should have saved it." Perhaps it was her adventurousness he disliked. But both my parents sought fulfillment in their own unique ways. And occasionally he came to my mom's club to hear a favorite band.

Old Town was a hippie haven, and full of tourists. I roamed the streets, meeting young people from all over. Under my mother's open canopy, we developed a more radical approach to society: marching against racism, protesting the war, trying out drugs, and challenging authority. My father was aghast. He tried to exert influence and set limits, but by that time we were having none of it. My parent's differences mirrored the greater societal conflicts emerging in the sixties, and we were caught in its web.

My dad tried hard to include us in his life, doing what he could to keep us entertained. My uncle Grady drove up from

Texas with two horses we kept at a stable near my father's work. For the winter time, he got a snowmobile. Eventually we took our horses up to a small ranch my father had bought in the Wisconsin hills. My sister moved up, and I followed after my school ended. My brother settled near us with his wife a few years later.

Our dreams were of a happy life in the country. And we did well for the first few years. However, my father's drinking increased. He worked as the bartender at a lounge out on Highway 14. When he came home, he often woke us up.

"Wake up and pee, the world's on fire!" he called out loudly. We were sleeping in a small open A-frame. The only door was to the bathroom.

A lovey-dovey drunk, he hugged and kissed us and wanted to talk. He was never inappropriate with me, though it always felt a bit creepy that he dated girls my age, including one named Bonnie.

I loved my father and he loved me. But his moral compass was a bit off-center. Once he took me for a ride on the tractor in order to steal a plowing tool from a neighbor. He had not mentioned his intention until we got to the neighbor's land. And he was critical. He demeaned my brother and his wife, poking fun at their propensity for collecting dogs and cats.

My mother strove to never speak badly of my father to us, but my father did not have such moral qualms. He uttered sharp barbs occasionally about her weight and her choices in men. Totally loyal to my mother, those criticisms did not sit well with me. Once I yelled, "I have to love you, but I don't have to like you!" as I slammed the door behind me and drove back to Chicago.

My experiences on the ranch were filled with beautiful, powerful moments: jumping our horses over hay bales, skinny dipping with my friends, raising animals, and the feeling of a family reunited. The love we shared was a heady brew. But nothing lasted forever and entropy began to take us down.

The discord in our family was becoming a problem, with no real resources for knowing how to resolve it. I reminded my brother, my sister and myself of dad's good qualities. It was when our grullo mare was killed by lightning, leaving her baby colt alone, that a sinking feeling filled me. Was that horrible accident a reflection of the deteriorating relationship between my father and us children?

When I moved to Madison, I carried pain deep within of anger, disappointment and failure. And I vowed to find a better world, with better people. People with moral fiber; people who knew how to deal with negative feelings. I needed to know there were better places out there. And I wanted to be better myself.

QUESTIONS

Why is not a question therapists usually ask. It can be too confrontative for their clients, triggering early memories of parents or teachers looming over them, "Why did you do that?" The spotlight of blame can wash out any wanted insight.

As well, the question why does not produce the type of results a therapist looks for. It is curt and commonly leads to a curt response. A therapist wants their client's story to unfold, not become a game of question and answer. How and what happened are more open-ended, allowing the storyteller room to spread.

When asked why I moved to a spiritual community, I faced a blank wall. But while writing this chapter, describing my earlier life, memories came that had slipped from my awareness. Many were painful. A picture emerged of a failed direction, where the best intentions were not enough.

Delving into one's history requires a curiosity. Questions become important tools in that search. A pat answer can be easily formulated, or one can begin a journey inward, exploring what happened and letting the understanding come slowly.

Most therapists use a lot of questions. At first my clients would tell their story factually, with minimal feeling. My curiosity helped them dig deeper, feel more. But sometimes the how *and the* what happened *would hang in the air, unanswered and unfelt. And that was fine with me. One has to be ready to re-experience unsettling memories. One has to feel safe enough.*

2

The Road Less Traveled

Staying Dogma-Free

I was in love with nature as a child, essentially a pagan at heart. My most blissful place at age five was the flower garden in my neighbor's backyard. Waves of rainbow hues moved through her beds over springtime: sky blue forget-me-nots, plush purple irises, and tall gladioli in rose, pink and delicate apricot. In the summer, sprays of yellow, orange and red dominated: brick-colored mums, black-eyed Susans, red asters and bright white daisies.

Seduced by the beauty, I snuck over often, moving slowly down the grassy paths. My fingers stroked the soft velvets; my face moved close to inhale the thick perfumes and look deep into each flower's cup. Most times the sun's light revealed a sparkling iridescence. Butterflies fluttered around me and bees hovered over each bud.

I imagined fairies and fauns dancing around the flowers, waking up buds in the spring and bedding the plants down in

13

the winter, like in the movie Fantasia. Lying on the grass, I was in my own kind of heaven. The Earth was a beautiful place to be.

A year later, my first grade catechism class taught me about the Catholic view of life. The nuns showed us pictures, framed in blue and edged in gold, of God, Jesus, and Mary. I imagined God as a kindly, old man on a throne of sunlight streaming through the clouds, lighting the greenery in our neighborhood.

I preferred going to church when it was empty. Then I could speak freely to God. My parents were not particularly religious and only decided to become Catholics to give their children a church to belong to. They attended mass and maintained the semblance for a few years, only to drop everything as their marriage fell apart. I continued to attend church services after their divorce. Getting to church was not always possible, so at times I held my own service in front of the crucifix in our hallway. My brother and sister snickered behind my back. I became 'the white sheep' of our family.

A strange event broadened my view of the spiritual world. In fourth grade a new girl joined our class. Madeline was slightly overweight, and I sensed she had some difficulties with confidence. We played together at recess and I invited her to my house. When she came, my mother greeted her with warmth and freshly baked cookies.

"I wish she were my mom," Madeline told me later.

Is your mother so bad? I wondered silently.

One Saturday, Madeline invited me to her birthday party. A birthday party, in our suburban town, meant food, games and prizes. We ran around her home, laughing and screaming. Her mother was watching from the kitchen, quick to get something when needed.

At one point, she came to my side.

"Bonnie, are you having fun?"

"Yes," I smiled.

"Good. Well, I wanted to meet you."

"Oh?" I became a bit uncomfortable, being singled out like this.

"Madeline really enjoys your friendship, and had a lot of fun visiting you. She also told me how wonderful your mother was to her," she explained.

I sensed something odd, like she needed me to reassure her. "I like her too," I offered.

Not sure what to say next, I began to slowly slide back into the melee.

She waved me off. "Yeah, go have fun."

After cake and ice cream, Madeline's mother handed out gift-wrapped packages. I watched in anticipation as my friends opened up their prizes: little tea sets, makeup kits, tiaras, and other toys. She came to me with a white-packaged lump. It rested heavy in my hand. I unwrapped the paper, revealing a ceramic Chinese man, shoulders slightly rounded, with a wide brim hat and floor length robe. He had long white hair and a beard, and carried a round sphere and a fan. I was surprised, and a bit shocked. What sort of prize was this?

"Do you like him?" My friend's mother came up behind me.

Quickly hiding any disappointment, I nodded and smiled.

"I got him at Chinatown in the city, and thought he would make a good party prize."

"Oh yes. Thank you." I wrapped him up quickly then looked around. No one else had received a similar gift.

On our way home, I sat in the back seat of our loaded car, my girlfriends buzzing with excitement, showing off their prizes. I envied them, for they could play, dress up and pretend to be a princess with their new toys. What could be played with my statue? Sheepishly unwrapping my gift, no one seemed to notice. As my fingers stroked the little figure's glazed form, I recognized something special in his humble stance and in the kindness of his soft features. At that moment, he became the best gift. I still have him with me, sixty odd years later. He has a chipped hat and sleeves, dirty face and hands, well-travelled. I doubt those tea sets have fared so well for so long.

My relationship to our church sputtered to a stop shortly after my parent's divorce. One Sunday, I attended mass with my best friend's family. The priest, who welcomed churchgoers, looked away despite my attempts to say hi. I believed he ignored me because of my parents' actions. I stopped going after that.

Another freeing occurred in school, during my religion class. Sister Eugenia, our teacher for seventh grade, spoke to us as budding grownups. "Talking about God as an old man on a throne of light is easier for younger children to understand. But you are old enough to think of God in a different way, as an ever present, but unseen Being, having no shape." Wrapping my thoughts around this different view of God took effort. How to imagine a shapeless entity? Eventually the image of an invisible presence replaced the enthroned being of light in my mind. My beliefs were becoming more spiritual.

Everything shifted when we moved into the city for my high school years. At first we lived in a small studio apartment next to my mother's blues club, and my days were spent roaming Wells Street, a tourist hangout. I was educated in the ways of the street, learning to avoid dangerous situations. I followed the local bands, went to parties and explored the world of drugs.

Despite this profane existence, my spiritual side continued to emerge. At one point, my mother, my sister and I shared a house with Pam, a folk singer friend of my mother's, and her two daughters, Iris and Jenny.

One morning, as I ironed my shirt, Iris, who was eleven, asked me, "Do you believe in witches?"

I set the iron upright to think about it. It seemed quite possible certain people might be able to exert force on the world by generating a deep intent to get what they wanted.

"I do think witchcraft is possible, but not like the show Bewitched, where a nose twitch makes something happen."

She nodded in agreement. "Well good, cause my mom and I are witches. We have certain powers."

"Oh," I replied, not knowing exactly what she meant, but always willing to give others the benefit of the doubt.

From then on, Pam began to share some of her world with me, and showed me her spell book. I listened cautiously, having decided one's motives must be pure when manipulating the material world. An event underlined that decision.

Once, late at night, I was riding in an empty CTA bus with a friend. We were clipping along at a fast pace. I loved moving through the air with the cool wind on me. Force from my belly blended with the speed; my will pushed the bus on and on, until, astonishingly, the driver drove through a red light. I was shocked. Did I influence the driver or was it a coincidence? Either way, I vowed never to do that again.

Through Pam, I met someone who opened a door for me, spiritually. One Saturday morning, we girls were lying on the floor in our living room, watching an old Charlie Chan movie. There was a knock and I got up to answer. A man stood outside, asking for Pam. As I looked up at him, I was stunned. His smile was gentle and he radiated kindness and compassion. A yearning filled me, an impulse to give up everything and follow him. I closed the door after our interchange, wondering if I had lost an opportunity. Later that day Pam told me about him. "He is the disciple of a teacher from India."

Pam must have spoken to him of my interest, for a few days later she placed in my hand a book he sent to me, entitled *The Path of the Masters*. It began with the introduction, "This book will find you only when you are ready." It described a spiritual world beyond the physical and a method of receiving spiritual knowledge through a teacher, whom one would find when the time was right. I never saw the man again, but the next step in my spiritual journey had been laid out.

Pam was a source of new understandings for me. And yet she had her problems. She started working as a psychologist at a psychiatric center by lying about her credentials, and was soon found out. She disappeared shortly afterwards, leaving her children with us. We never heard from her again. Eventually Iris and Jenny's father retrieved them.

Years later I happened to hear Pam on a cassette tape. She established herself as a Native American teacher of herbology, though she seemed to have garnered a reputation online for deceit, claiming to be part of a tribe she did not actually belong to. My mother's respect for her was gone, yet I could not view her in a totally negative light. She had expanded my world-view, and I was grateful.

STAYING DOGMA-FREE

It is best to not be too tight-fisted about one's beliefs. For in the swirl of differing ideas, a larger awareness can emerge.

My views of God/Spirit, life, and myself have always been shifting and growing. I tried on various paths like clothing, wearing them as long as I benefitted from their teachings. Then, when another perspective presented itself, I expanded my beliefs, tearing the seams of the old 'til the limiting cloth had to be discarded. Having faith was easy for me, for every path contained nuggets of truth and expressions of love, but I learned early not to cling to dogma.

A truth-seeker's path requires a willingness to throw out the rigid and make way for a more flexible view. It can be uncomfortable to disturb the settled understandings in our mind. We gain strength from a belief system, find a stability in well-defined teachings. Yet, a more inclusive perspective moves us one step closer to the wider reality. One of the lesser known of the three maxims found over the entrance to the temple of Apollo at Delphi is "Beware False Certainty," a warning for all truth-seekers.

By the time I left the Catholic Church, the teachings seemed overly structured and limited. And yet Jesus shared an important message I took to heart, that of love.

3

Finding My Purpose

Purpose

The winter break of 1967 was a pivotal moment for me. The year before had unfolded like a nativity calendar, every month a new experience. It was sandwiched between blizzards. The first was the record setting blizzard that stopped Chicago's movement for days. My family and my mother's friends hunkered down at our house during that storm. Playing games and cooking meals, we waited out the city's standstill. Going to get more supplies, my sister and I walked through cliffs of white. Spotting an antenna was the only way we knew whether we were on the sidewalk or on top of a car.

I became sixteen that year. My best friend, Robin, and I often talked late into the night. We read existential literature, listened to Sgt. Peppers Lonely Hearts Club Band, and memorized Simon and Garfunkel songs. Our first LSD trip happened that winter. In the summer, we attended the Human Be-In, a weekend music festival in Lincoln Park. I sported prism glasses and wore a dress created from a pale green bedsheet sprinkled with silver sparkles.

Bu and I obsessed about the world of Tolkien and established a hobbit hole in our basement. She loved animals, and brought a pair of squirrels to our house, while one recovered from injuries. Another time she was given a baby raccoon. Coony Rac joined our family until his hormones kicked in, making life with him intolerable.

Life was an adventure that year and my creativity sparked with aliveness.

In the fall, I returned to high school as a Junior while Robin started college. None of my friends at school had entered my inner sanctuary as Robin had. Multiple friends, yet none who went to the depths exploring what life meant, as she and I had done. I was lost without her. Little bouts of sadness began to creep in.

At the end of '67, during the Christmas break, another blizzard held us hostage. I retreated to my room, holed up with Hermann Hesse's *Siddhartha* and *Zen Flesh, Zen Bones*. Spiraling slowly into my self, I questioned my life. All that had excited me before, felt meaningless.

What began as faint murmurings and doubts, built up in intensity over a few days. My inner questions pounded repeatedly in my mind. I wrote them on the wall in big letters. *Why am I here? What is important enough for me to stay in this life?* I paced the floor, caught in my thoughts.

Do I stay or do I go?

It was not as if a suicide was an option. I just needed some reason to keep on going. It was vitally important to figure this one out.

My mother questioned my sanity after she saw the wall. "Are you okay?"

"Yeah, I am, mom. I'm fine."

Somehow she knew it was true and left me to it.

I lay on my bed, imagining my self as a building, whose bricks comprised the aspects of my life. Friendships, knowledge, family, creativity, all experiences up until now, did not seem important enough to base my life around, to build a self around. My take-away from reading Buddhist texts was no thing was constant, no thing could be relied upon to always be there. No person, no idea, no creation would last long enough to provide me a foundation, a reason for moving forward.

After tearing away all the ephemeral bricks of my life, my mind became empty space. I floated there for a brief time. Surprisingly, from that space an answer emerged. The most important reason, the only reason to stay was for love. Love made my struggles in life worthwhile. Love was the glue that connected us all. I chose love to be the cornerstone of my building, and guide my decisions. A deep purpose was forged inside me that day.

In my late 20's I was reminded of that purpose. While living in Madison, I helped start a group called the Fellowship of the Rainbow. We planned to establish a community, and began looking for land. Joe, our leader, valued people who had psychic abilities, and had invited two women who channeled and the husband of one of the women, to join us. I was excited and looked forward to knowing them better.

A few months after joining, they withdrew from our group, after having a disagreement with Joe. It was very hush, hush, but

I was disappointed. They would have been important in helping us create the community, and I was enamored by their ability to receive messages from disincarnate beings.

Soon afterwards Jane, one of the three, called me.

"We were talking and realized we really liked you and wondered if you'd like to join our group?"

Wow! I was a bit shocked, and knew to give it some time before giving my answer. Leaving my group would not be easy. We had been together for a few years. Barely knowing the three was not an incentive, but the gift of their request and my own curiosity kept the idea of joining them circling in my thoughts. I went through weeks of indecision, going back and forth. First favoring the Fellowship, then desire to explore the possibilities of the new group would rise up to complicate things again.

One overcast day, I walked to work through the UW campus. Still in a muddle about which way to go, my mind was exhausted. I reached the top of a hill overlooking the lake and stopped to gaze off into the distance. The sound of the waters and the cool breeze soothed my thinking. My brain stopped its spin and a knowing rose up. The knowing felt like a strong current, forming a huge pillar of energy running through me from the earth to the sky. *Love, I have to choose Love.* From that point on, everything fell into place. I knew I would stay with the Fellowship and would say no to Jane. A clarity came with the pillar and lasted for weeks. Knowing one's purpose at such a deep level can be a powerful tool, an awakening tool.

I wasn't sure of the right way to tell Jane. When she called my words stumbled. I closed down my confused thoughts and simply pushed out the words of my truth, "I have to choose Love." I repeated it more strongly. "I have to choose Love, and that means staying with the Fellowship." Why it meant that was unclear, I just knew it was true.

I dodged a bullet that day. The glamour of having psychic friends was frivolous, not a reason to join.

Practicing love was not always an easy task. In my early 30's, I worked as a unit secretary in the Trauma and Life Support Center of the University Hospital. My supervisor came in one morning, followed by a pretty, smiling girl. "Suzanna is new. Would you train her here?"

"Of course," I said and set up a chair for her next to me. We got along well until her flippant and cavalier attitude presented problems. I caught her applying nail polish as she talked to an anxious family member, who had just heard their loved one was in the ICU. The nurses in the unit quietly complained to me about her.

It was she I worked on to love. Every time critical thoughts came up, I countered with thoughts of why she might be that way. Her emotional intelligence seemed to be lacking. But none of us knew her past. Perhaps she was raised in a family that cared about image more than substance. My heart slowly warmed to her. My efforts paid off. The well of love I developed deepened, and flowed freely when I was with her. And my acceptance seemed to do wonders for her work performance.

PURPOSE

I doubt many people truly question why they are here in this life. They just get on with living. And if they do seek an answer, it is bound to be a personal one, because we each have our own direction.

It's fascinating to meet someone who knew from childhood they would become a musician or a doctor. Most of us ride the train of life without clearly knowing our destination.

As a therapist, I often asked my clients' purposes, usually for the decisions they made. Training oneself to look a little deeper has value. The more we analyze our reasonings, the better we understand ourselves. Then our choices become easier to make.

Sometimes smaller purposes can lead to the recognition of an overarching life direction. It may take time to formulate. It may be a vague quality such as love was for me, rather than a specific vision. But the more we ask, the more we look, the closer we get to what can truly motivate us in this life.

Once we grasp our purpose, we can sift the meaning of an experience through the lens of it. At times we are tempted to stray. On that hill overlooking Madison's lake, my soul had to step in to remind me.

4

A Divine Discontent

Discontent

*It has been called a divine discontent, the pressure from within
that makes one look for an ever-fleeting happiness and sense of
spiritual connection.*

In my twenties, I was always searching, reading of others'
journeys and visiting spiritual groups. All pointed the way to
the same goal, to a connection with God, and ultimately to a
connection with my soul. Encircling that goal, I was entranced
by the jewels of knowledge scattered along the various paths, but
never dared or even knew how to dare take the first steps in.

Practicing meditation was the one tool that helped me get
closer. The practice soothed the ragged edges of my anxiety,
and was a much needed respite from the stressors of my day. At
times, when meditating, a sparkling energy coursed through my
body, revitalizing me.

My early twenties were spent collecting experiences, a wide

range of experiences: different jobs, classes, travels and friends. And I dabbled in the world of relationships. My ideas for a career changed from nursing to psychology to horticulture. A sleeping bag was my constant bedding, for I was always on the move.

It was fun. Yet as the years wore on, my settle-down clock began ticking. I landed a job at the University Hospital in Madison, Wisconsin, and moved into a collective living situation, a large house rented by seven of us.

Early on in Madison, while browsing through books at the East-West Bookstore, I bumped into Marcus, a friend of one of my roommates. As we chatted, he took a paperback book off the shelf, *The Magic of Findhorn* by Paul Hawken.

"Have you heard of the Findhorn community?" he asked. "They grow huge vegetables by working with nature spirits."

Intrigued, I bought the book, intending to read it eventually. Slowly it moved to the back of my must-read book queue.

Anxiety and depression slipped through the cracks of my adventurous spirit in my later twenties. After receiving a Bachelor of Arts, I floundered. What to do next? Some vague idea of working in psychology filtered through my thinking, yet how could I make that happen? It was time to start creating my own life, commit to a concrete goal, establish a career and more permanent relationships. But to me everything felt a bit empty. Most of my friends seemed satisfied with the status quo, not interested in looking deeper.

Our house was at first a stimulating and exciting place to live. Two of my roommates were followers of a Sufi sect, and our conversations were brilliant. They moved on and other unique people joined us. Yet over the years, the place became another dead end for me. I fell into a silent war with one of my housemates over the timing of his piano playing. And my dating life had ground to a halt. I clung to my bedroom and slipped into a depressed state. How does one face a new stage of life when so unhappy?

As a student of astrology, I knew that our first Saturn Return, around the twenty-eighth year, was important. Before then, most people bumbled around in various jobs and living arrangements, figuring out what they didn't want to spend the rest of their lives doing. The Return kicked off another twenty-eight year cycle of establishing oneself in the community and making life commitments to, commonly, a career, marriage and children. For me, it was not worth settling down when so disconnected from my soul. I needed to find a spiritual path to invest myself in. My search began in earnest.

In Madison, I discovered an Edgar Cayce study group. Edgar Cayce was a clairvoyant who received medical suggestions for patients while in a trance. After reading his biography, I trusted in his integrity and the authenticity of his gifts. Joining a group that shared an interest in his teachings was an easy fit. Yet I stayed a member for a couple years only. Our plans to eventually form a community were waveringly unsteady. And I wasn't sure a community in Wisconsin was where I needed to be.

A group of ex-Findhorn members, the Lorians, had moved to Madison. The group included David Spangler, a mystic and spiritual teacher, who was also one of the co-leaders of the Findhorn community about ten years earlier. They offered a series of workshops, and I immediately signed up.

Their teachings had a spiritual wisdom while being ultimately practical. One important lesson was around earth changes: earthquakes, volcanic eruptions and weather anomalies. Edgar

Cayce's readings referred to them, and many people in New Age circles planned with these catastrophes in mind. David approached those predictions in a different way. "It's important to not give energy to destructive visions, but strive to stay focused on a positive view."

The Lorians eventually moved on, but Findhorn loomed larger in my thoughts. I finally pulled out *The Magic of Findhorn* and began reading.

The story of how the community came to be was hard to believe. The three founders, Peter Caddy, Eileen Caddy and Dorothy Maclean, had no intention of creating a community. They simply followed, step by step, their inner guidance, which led them in 1962 to a small caravan (a travel trailer) situated in the Findhorn Bay Caravan Park, in Scotland. The area was mostly sand dunes, next to the North Sea.

Eileen, who was very traditional, was surprised to hear a "still, small voice within" begin speaking to her years earlier. When the three moved into the caravan park, she received explicit directions. They were to stay there, despite little savings and no job prospects. To supplement their meager income from the government, Peter began a garden the next Spring. They all contributed to transforming a sand dune, with a layer of grass turf on the surface, to a suitable bed for radishes and lettuce greens. Seaweed, manure, and flipped turf chunks created that first garden.

Shortly afterwards, Dorothy's inner voice suggested she connect in meditation with the essential beings of nature, such as the essence of the wind, of the sea and of different types of plants. Peter, ever practical, asked her to focus on communicating with the essences (or Devas as Dorothy called them) of the vegetables he was growing, thinking to get help for his garden. He asked specific questions and she received answers that Peter implemented, resulting in plants of enormous size and vitality.

Eileen's guidances were published and attracted like-minded people to join them. But it was the garden that brought the attention of the general public. People travelled to northern Scotland just to see the place, and the BBC filmed a documentary there. Soon guests wanted to stay, and the caravan park began to fill.

When the community was first developing, Peter, who loved to travel and meet new people, invited an elder Scotsman to visit. Robert Ogilvy Crombie (called ROC for short) was a Renaissance man, a scientist who explored music, the dramatic arts and philosophy. ROC had heard Peter talk at a gathering of the Scottish UFO Society.

Shortly after, ROC was walking in the botanical gardens in Edinburgh and sat on a bench near his favorite tree. On a hill, the city unfolded before him in the distance. Suddenly he felt the atmosphere thicken and noticed a small being with cloven hooves and tiny horns flitting from plant to plant. It was a nature spirit.

The being danced around and then plopped in front of the bench, curiously watching him.

ROC leaned forward. "Hello."

The faun-like creature leapt back in surprise, then approached. "Can you see me?"

"Yes I do see you." ROC was just as surprised.

ROC's relationship with nature spirits developed over the weeks that followed. He believed his sudden ability to penetrate the unseen world had purpose, connected with Peter Caddy's garden.

A special relationship with nature was developing at Findhorn, a co-creative experiment with the potential to be an example for mankind. Each person brought an essential contribution to the formation of the garden and the community that was to follow. Peter was skilled in using his will to manifest his vision in developing the garden, and later the buildings and other structures of the community. Eileen brought in her guidance from God, which led the group step-by-step. Dorothy contributed her messages from the formative, more angelic realms of nature, the Devas.

ROC brought in a fourth element, the realm of what is called the elementals. He became the go-between the community and the nature spirits, speaking on how to cooperate together to work with their beloved plants. Peter was also warned by ROC when he planned to do something offensive to the nature spirits, such as cutting down an old thicket of brambles that were flowering at the time.

David Spangler, a fifth major influence, came to the community in 1970 and brought a vision of education just when the visitor numbers were increasing. Lessons in co-creation with nature were one of the classes offered.

For an idealist such as myself, this was a story too good to be true. The nature spirits described by ROC were happy, laughing and singing as they worked; as happy as I was at five, lying in my neighbor's yard, surrounded by flowers.

I decided to go to Scotland, thinking to stop at Findhorn first, then continue my search at other communities until I found the right one for me. My grandfather passed, leaving me a small, but perfect sum of money. My sister bought a car with her inheritance, and enrolled in a nursing program. I bought a ticket to Scotland and had enough money to stay on, if it felt right.

I set about making reservations for the early part of March. After booking a cheap flight to London, I quit my job, left my friends, and moved into my mother's apartment in Chicago. We celebrated Christmas together as I made preparations for my trip.

DISCONTENT

Discontent is a great motivator. Coming from within, it causes our course to alter. Instead of a well-lit path before us, it is a boot to the backside, forcing a step into the unknown. If perfectly satisfied, one would never change. Dissatisfaction is the inner push, engaging the outer search that leads onward. For many people, it is all they need to make a move.

But for others, discontent is not enough. I learned from my clients that people can tolerate a lot of stuckness before making a change. Safety trumps the possibility of greater happiness for them. There are no guarantees one will emerge into a better place. And truthfully, not everybody does.

In my initial intake with a client, I wanted to know what boot kicked them into action. I would ask, "What brought you here today?"

Their responses covered a gamut of reasons: "I'm depressed," "I lost my job," "I've always wanted to start counseling."

I'd continue, "But why now? What happened to actually get you to make the call?"

It was then I heard what motivated them: an ultimatum from their wife, increasing symptoms, a close shave with death. For most, an overwhelming event or an uncontrollable problem forced them to seek help. Seldom was it for their own growth. As soon as the pressures let up, many were ready to leave therapy. Yet some knew a deeper change was needed, and stayed the course for longer.

It's not easy to step out of one's safe place. Discontent is the push one likely needs behind finding a therapist or leaving home for an unknown community.

5

The Power of Choice

Decision or Choice

I looked for a place to belong, and perhaps the thought of a place hid from me the greater truth. Eventually I would find home lay within me, rather than in the stones and wood of a place. But going to Findhorn was a first step, and even in taking that step, my resolve was tested.

I thought myself clever, scheduling a cheap flight to London from Ohio. Ohio was a five hour car trip from Chicago. My sister offered to take me, as long as we shared driving. Setting out the morning of the flight, we headed south through Indiana before turning east. The skies were grey with snow forecasted, but the dry highway snaking through the wintered landscape was a hopeful sign.

At the top of one of many hills, we saw a large river valley. The bridge below us glistened with ice, as did the road. Strewn about were twenty or thirty vehicles that had slid down the hill and piled up at the bottom.

"Oh shit!" I said as we began to slide straight towards the pileup. I pumped on the brakes cautiously, knowing we would lose control if they locked up. As we neared, I had two options, either aim for the car in front of us, or the metal barricades that kept cars from falling into the river. I gambled on the barricades, approaching at a slight angle that rubbed the side of our vehicle, but also slowed us down. The people in front of us watched helplessly as we slid to a stop, missing their vehicle by a few feet. We, just as helpless, watched the next car as they slid towards us. A hit meant we would have to stay at the scene, and probably miss my flight. Luckily, they found a way to avoid us, angling off to the left.

Assuming we were trapped, I walked through the massing of cars and jack-knifed trailers and realized there was a path our little Honda could fit through. My sister started up the engine and inched her way forward, weaving between vehicles. The other drivers watched as we made it to the open road.

The weather got worse the further south we went. The snow blew across the highway and began to accumulate. It was when we turned east that I questioned whether we could make it. The driving wind blew the flakes against the windshield and blinded our view. We could see only a few feet in front of the car. Still determined, I pushed forward as the blizzard pushed back.

After ten minutes of driving, visibility at almost zero, we pulled into a truck stop, joining a group gathered there, waiting for a break in the weather. We learned the conditions would continue until way after the flight was scheduled to depart.

"Okay, I give up!" I said to my sister. "Let's turn back."

Amazingly, traveling in the same direction as the prevailing winds made our visibility perfect. Our return trip to Chicago was obstacle free.

Basking in the warmth and security of my mother's apartment, I questioned my plan. *Am I making the right choice?* It felt as if a giant hand had held me back, like nature was warning me, "don't go!"

I called an airline and reserved a seat on a more expensive flight to London. All the while my stomach churned with indecision. Losing hundreds of dollars by missing my flight, now hundreds more were required to make my scheduled workshop on time. Going to Scotland by myself was a bold move, heading into the unknown. *Is this crazy?* Nature seemed to be cautioning me. And my mother's home felt so cozy and safe. Yet I couldn't just give up. My mind raced as I grappled with the choice.

The day of the flight, packed and waiting, I paced the floor, trying to shake off my nerves. The apartment was empty. I had said my goodbye's the night before, yet was still undecided. *Dear God, should I go? What is the right choice here? Tell me what to do.* The clock ticked. No answer came. No clue was given. Finally, just as I needed to leave to catch my flight, something fell into place in my gut area.

"I'm going, no matter what!" No one else heard, just me. Rising up, I strapped on my backpack and headed out the door. Although a wintery day, the street was lit by the sun, the air warm. As I walked to the station, smiling people nodded hello. The words *sunshine*, *golden*, and *lovely* streamed past on billboards outside the window of the elevated train. It was as if the world celebrated with me, celebrated my bravery in making a hard choice.

Having missed a night of sleep, I was groggy when we landed in London the next morning. The underground took me to King's Cross station where I bought a bus ticket to Edinburgh. The skinny sidewalks around the area were clear indicators this was another country. I ordered coffee at a corner coffee shop while waiting for the bus to depart. Hoping for a large cup of steaming brew to warm my fingers around, the server brought a demitasse filled with a thick, bitter liquid and a small pitcher of cream, my first exposure to French-style espresso coffee. It was delicious!

Sleeping in fits and starts on the bus, my arrival in Edinburgh was quickly followed by a train to Inverness. A young American woman, also on her way to Inverness, sat next to me. She planned to stay at the youth hostel and suggested I get a bed there as well.

The hostel was set in a large grey stone building close to the River Ness. The owner asked me a few carefully worded questions about my plans, and sold me a resident membership right on the spot, so I could pay less for my stay. It was a practice frowned upon by the Scottish Youth Hostel Organization. But the owner, clearly a believer in thriftiness, wanted to save me some money.

Dropping off my pack, I left to explore the city, walking along the riverside. Loch Ness, where the famous monster was sighted, was a few miles upstream. I bought a thick wool sweater at one of the shops, to stave off the biting cold. Warm again, I roamed the pavered streets.

That evening, we went to the nearest pub to get a meal.

The pub was filled with rousing laughter and drinks spilling all around. It was Friday, payday, and time to celebrate. We were welcomed and questioned about our journeys, garnering boisterous but respectful male attention.

The next morning I caught the train to Forres.

Descending from the car at my destination, I was unsure where to go. It was a blustery March day, the wind spinning the snow as if on a mission, icy bullets striking my face and hands. Grateful for my new sweater, I zipped up my windbreaker to deflect the assault. It was then I noticed a grinning, balding man standing in front of a small white bus, with the name HAMISH printed on a placard on its back fender. He called out for anyone going to the Findhorn community to hop aboard.

Putting my backpack in the rear, I climbed in, noting the others from our train. Their rainbow colored scarves and hats gave them away, contrasting sharply with the sedate grays and plaids commonly worn by the Scots.

Before we set off, the man addressed us.

"Welcome to the Findhorn Community. I'm David. You are in for a unique experience. I suggest you stay open to what life brings you while here."

An American, I noted, then repeated under my breath, "stay open." My whole trip had been about staying open, especially the act of courage required to start me off.

David drove us through the middle of Forres. Shops outlined the central square and clock tower, all built with grey stone. We took a right to climb a hill, then entered a long tree-covered driveway, which opened to reveal a large grey stone mansion. People were sitting out on the picnic tables in front of the building, chatting despite the brisk winds. The bus stopped on a circular parking area. As I stepped down, my gaze followed the expanse of green in front of the building. We were on the edge of a hill. Across the road was a golf course, and in the distance the fields and hills rose into mountains.

I entered a glassed-in vestibule, lined with plants and luggage. A wide staircase rose up at the far end and halls crossed left and right. This was Cluny Hill College, formerly a four-star hotel, and earlier, in the beginning of the century, a health spa. The picture in the brochure sent to me months before, showed a four-storied, castle-like structure, with grey stone facades rising high along its roofline.

What surprised me most upon entering this building was the welcome I felt, a warmth in my belly. *It feels like home.* Over the next few weeks, I wondered if this was the right place for me.

The foyer was busy, with people coming and going. While waiting at the reception desk, I noticed a person sitting on a step of the staircase and another behind, massaging her shoulders. More people joined, creating a massage chain that led up to the top of the stairs. Clearly spontaneity was welcome here.

Across from reception was a spacious common room with groupings of chairs and low tables. A large bay window overlooked the front garden, encircled by overstuffed chairs and tables laden with newspapers. People, talking or reading, were sprinkled around the room.

I found my group leaders, Buffy, from New Zealand, and Sean, from Ireland, who checked me in. My room would be ready after lunch. Evidently, Housekeeping was still busy making beds and cleaning up. Saturday was transition day at Cluny, when people from the previous week's workshops left and people for the next week arrived. I put my backpack in a cloak room, and followed the hallway to the dining room, hungry after my morning's scurry to get there.

The room was spacious and elegant, lined with windows, paneled walls and a thick red carpet. I walked into a cloud of noise, from groups of people gathered at the many tables around the room.

Not knowing a soul, I grabbed some food from the buffet table and sat near the door, keeping my focus on my meal. So many conversations around the room was intense, but I wished I could listen in. After lunch, I took my pack up to the room.

My roommates were already there, two middle-aged women from Germany, Maia and Cordula. They had come together to attend the Experience Week, which is the weeklong introductory course everyone is required to take. Afterwards they would stay for the two-week workshop on spiritual development I had also signed up for. *My roommates for the duration.*

A little disappointed, I hoped to have roommates closer to my age. We were at very different stages of life. Yet, over the next three weeks I learned how lovely they were, and helpful as I adjusted to this new world.

DECISION OR CHOICE?

As a therapist, I've watched my clients struggle with decision-making. Often they evaded the act altogether, letting the pieces fall as they may. It's one way to avoid the haunting question, "did I decide right?"

As we weigh our options, wavering back and forth, we may still not find the best answer. The mental gymnastics one goes through can be exhausting. Commonly, we seek expert opinions, or an authority to tell us what to do. I suggested to my indecisive clients, "Imagine choosing one, and see how you feel. Do you weaken or feel stronger? What other clues tell you whether this is the right decision?"

In my experience, choosing is different than deciding. It's powerful, comes from our gut. Our will makes the choice, not our mind. When we mentally decide, not a lot of our being goes into it. But choosing from our gut area is like a canon shot of energy. Nothing ultimately gets in our way.

It is interesting how the environment circles around our choice or lack of. When indifferent, we meander down the roadway. But when late for something important, have you ever noticed the lights changing and traffic moving aside to let you stream through?

Going to Findhorn was a mental decision I made early on. The strength of my decision dissipated over the months, as my fears grew. My drive to Ohio was riddled with obstacles, and my own doubts. Yet after making the choice from my gut area, the way cleared and my surroundings shined with light, supporting me.

I've made few true choices in my life. Most of my decisions have been less important. But when I have made a choice, such as saying yes to my husband's proposal, it came from a depth within, as if it carried a soul's purpose behind it. That is how I know I've made the right choice.

6

Experiencing the New; Releasing the Old

Vulnerability

A lump was growing in my throat. I started my Experience Week excited and open. But by Monday, I was on overload. Each new experience stirred up my insides. Taken deeper into the crucible that Findhorn was known for, I was not prepared for the intensity of my reactions to the place.

The Beechtree room, where our workshop met, was a large space with thirty chairs placed in a circle. At its center a candle flickered inside a flower wreath. The room was filled with people, young and old, chatting in small groups.

I was nervous and grabbed onto my seat, to steady my hands. A few deep breaths helped settle my stomach.

The workshop focalizers (a word used in place of leader, to imply they held the focus for the group) started the meeting with an "attunement." Standing up, we held hands with our eyes closed, creating a circle of connection.

Buffy spoke softly. "Let's release all that brought us to this point... all expectations... and simply be here in this present moment, with each other."

After a brief silence, the hand squeeze sent around the circle told us we were done. We all sat down.

They covered the logistics first: baths, schedules for meals and meditation. Then we were asked to share our reasons for coming. I learned most of the group were from a European country, and a sprinkling came from South Africa, Australia, New Zealand, Canada, South America and the US. Some had followed an intuitive feel of rightness, many were curious, and others knew of the community from friends and family. A few had travelled together; most came alone. One man was fairly guarded, not really believing this place could be something special for him. I understood his doubt. The 'magic' described in the books was hard to believe.

As my turn drew close, I tried to focus on the others' stories rather than plan my own. Not an easy task, with my stomach lightly spinning. I had never spoken to such a large group before.

"I've read a lot of spiritual books and looked for a path for me, but never found one. After meeting the Lorians, I wondered if Findhorn might be the right place."

The words came out a shade monotone and distant. Next time, I intended to do better.

Following the sharing, we broke for tea. A table outside the dining room had hot drinks and cookies. The tea table would be a godsend for me over the week, a welcome break from the intensity of people, ideas and my own emerging feelings.

In the second half of the afternoon, we picked jobs. I chose

Park Housekeeping. Monday morning the bus would take me to the Park where I'd join the Housekeeping team. Working a part of each day provided the opportunity to get to know the community members better.

Finally, we toured the building, first going to the Cluny Sanctuary, originally a chapel. Mostly used for silent meditation or prayer, we could do any practice that did not interfere with another's. Yoga or chanting was best done elsewhere. I peeked inside. A double row of chairs encircled a candle in the center of the room. The cathedral-like ceiling was outlined in exposed wood beams. A large window at the end allowed rays of sunlight in. To enter we were to take off our shoes, and many wrapped in a blanket for sitting in the cold space. Neatly piled near the entry were a stack of yellow wool blankets.

I loved the smooth, organized feel of Cluny. It was like a tiny town, with a sauna, a library and a small shop. At one end of the building was a glass-enclosed ballroom. Across from it a cave of a room, complete with a mirrored bar and a pink carpet scrolled with dark bubbles. It spoke of a time of cocktails and dancing when the building was a hotel. Out the back was a scruffy looking tennis court and an empty pool. In the underbelly of the building dwelt a laundry and the Boutique, a closet where one could find or leave used clothing. 'Shopping' in there would turn out to be a small travel adventure, as people left clothing sourced from countries across the globe.

We were told Cluny's connection to the community started when Peter was hired to manage the hotel in 1957. Peter, Eileen and Dorothy took on the struggling hotel, raising it to four-star status over the five years they worked there. Eileen's guidance was used for all the hotel decisions. They believed they would stay indefinitely, but that was not to be. Peter was transferred to another hotel, despite Eileen's prediction that Cluny would be part of their future. It was in 1976 that the community actually bought the hotel for 50,000 pounds, after the property had deteriorated enough to be affordable. It supplied workshop spaces and much needed housing for increasing numbers of guests.

After the afternoon session, I joined the meditation before dinner. Grabbing a blanket, I wrapped myself up and entered the cold, darkened room. The light of a candle guided me to an empty chair. Closing my eyes, I tried to settle my mind down. The person leading the meditation kept it very simple, ringing a bell to start, and adding a little 'food for thought' to kick off the twenty minutes of quiet.

Meditating since my early twenties, my quiet time was needed pretty much every day. Sometimes I reached a deep calm. Most of the time settling my mind was difficult, as was true this day. So much to think about. As my body relaxed, I became aware of a lump growing in my throat. First day and already I was that stressed.

Sunday morning we met in the ballroom to do Sacred Dance, led by a community member. The dances sourced from various countries and traditions. They were mostly done in a circle, hands linked together. Weaving slowly to Pachelbel's Canon was the highlight for me. Other dances required complicated footwork. The more I stumbled through the steps, the more I laughed with the others.

Every so often the thought popped up, *I want to stay here.* I countered it with, *of course I'll return home. I must go back.* My inner debate was beginning.

That afternoon we bussed four miles to the caravan park, the original site for the community. The land had been transformed from sand dunes into a lush garden of trees, bushes and perennials interspersed with buildings and caravans. Previously used as part of an airbase, the old runways on the property had been converted into a caravan park. The community recently bought the land and the caravan business, funded by donations from previous guests and friends from around the globe.

The Park Sanctuary was our first stop. Eileen had received the guidance to build a simple room that could seat about seventy-five people, with no decorations except the weaving of a sunrise hanging on a wall and the ever present candlelight in the center. The Community Center was the second building Eileen was given guidance about. The kitchen was built large enough to serve 200 people. The dining room started small, and had been expanded multiple times as the population of the community grew.

The grey stone Park Building had been donated to the community by a friend. It provided rooms for offices, a library and meeting spaces. The Publications building had a printing machine and stored many of the community's published books. The Phoenix, a shop for snacks, meat and new age trinkets, was located near the commercial caravan park. Besides the rentals, other caravans were scattered around the land, homes for members and guests. Cullerne, a large estate next to the Park, was farmed to grow vegetables.

A broad pentagon-shaped building, called the Universal Hall, was large enough to house the whole community for meetings and performances. I had heard about this building from the movie, *My Dinner with Andre*. Andre mentioned

Findhorn and in particular the Hall. He said the roof was built to allow quick removal in preparation for a UFO landing. The tour guide dispelled the story; the roof was solidly attached to the walls.

Pineridge was a piece of land set a short distance from the center of the community. Members' caravans, a day care center and craft studios were surrounded by a pine forest. A path from there wound past the pines and through sand dunes to the beaches of the North Sea.

The Park area had become a little village over the years, benefitting from creative ventures, additions and donations.

By the end of the second day, I could feel my shoulders tensing. That night I dreamed of *a grotesquely fat woman stuffed into a can. She hated being in there, but I was afraid releasing her would unleash a lot of anger and vengefulness. Although she was suffering, I chose to ignore her.* When I shared my dream with Maia and Cordula, it was not hard to connect it's meaning to the rise of pressure I felt and my tightening throat.

Monday morning was our first work day. I ate breakfast, then caught the bus to meet with members of the Park Housekeeping Department. There were five of us. After introductions and a brief attunement, available jobs were doled out. I chose to work in the laundry, preferring the simplicity of folding linens in a warm room.

That afternoon, we again met in the ballroom, this time to play games, led by our smiling bus driver, David. The games clearly had a purpose, to increase our trust in one another and find ways to work as a team. For one game we massed together, then grabbed random hands to create a knot. As a group, we were to work out how to unwind ourselves without releasing the hands we held.

Each evening we shared how we were doing. Over time the evening check-ins became easier for me. I felt more present in my sharing. But I did not share the stress I was feeling, the pressure building up as I absorbed more experiences. The lump in my throat grew and below my neck my insides felt blocked. I was not alone. Others in our group told me of their own struggles.

After sharing, a member came in to talk about an aspect of the community. The spiritual life at Findhorn was the first topic. We were told the community had no particular dogma and attracted people of various religions and practices. While we might pray to different beings or just believe in different approaches, what linked us was the same Spirit underlying them all.

Other topics included nature, the organizational structure, and living in community. One sharing particularly impressed me. Charlie, an Australian who had been around since the 70's, spoke of the organizational dynamics. Decisions were made by consensus. Wow! I was so tired of dealing with people in power, and working in hierarchical systems. Here was a place where my opinion would be heard, and included in the decision. I loved that.

As well, Charlie reminded us the members were not perfect. They would not always do the right thing. And yet, we could trust that each person tried their best. If expecting perfect fairness and love from those on a spiritual path, one will be disappointed when they fail to live up to our dream. Charlie's comment kicked that fantasy far away.

My debate between staying and going home became more pronounced over the week. One evening I dreamt: *My brother let me know my parents had died. The grief I felt was overwhelming. Being at Findhorn, I had not been informed in time and missed my chance to see them. Guilt feelings propelled me to return home.*

On Friday, the last day of the workshop, the day began with me reflecting on the terrible state I was in.

"I feel dead inside and the lump in my throat continues to throb," I told Cordula.

She was a graphologist, and had understood some things about me through my handwriting. "You have a strong will, initiative and intellect. But emotionally, you are repressing yourself."

I had been so mentally on edge over the week that meditating had been hopeless. This morning in the sanctuary, I pleaded, *"Please help me, God."* And for the first time since I had come, my throat relaxed and my shoulder muscles dropped. Energies flowed through my body again, waking up my heart and gut.

At lunch I spoke to Christine, a member of our group from London. I told her my dream of the fat lady. "I had been so shut down I felt dead inside. I guess I've been afraid to show my emotions; wanting to keep it all under control."

She had struggled with a similar challenge. "I now think of my feelings as a perceptual tool, giving me important bits of information, rather than as a threat to others."

Framing emotions in a more useful light helped. I was able to stop clenching and allow vulnerability in. My gut area quivered, alive again. During our last sharing, I told the group of my struggle, shedding all my barriers.

The focalizers then led us in an Angel Card meditation. I had wondered what the ring of small rectangular cards, encircling the central candle, was for. They were laid face-side down. After entering a quiet, receptive state, we were to draw one. The angel I picked was RELEASE. Accompanying the word was the drawing of a mother angel waving goodbye to her children in a school bus. I teared up, stunned by how perfect that card was.

Saturday arrived, the day of endings and new beginnings. Many of those I had connected with were going home, or elsewhere. So many hugs, so many goodbyes. I was sad to lose them. Afterwards, I joined a gathering of people in the front foyer to help the Housecare Department change sheets, vacuum and clean the bedrooms. As we attuned I thought of where I was now and where I had been a week ago, just entering through those doors.

It was a busy start to what turned out to be a rather lonely weekend.

VULNERABILITY

"Vulnerability is our best defense," is a phrase often used at Findhorn. For many people around the world, it would be hard to imagine that could be true. Vulnerability is seen as a liability, or a luxury, not often indulged in.

Many of us approach a social situation masked up, shielding ourself from possible criticism. Yet if we accept our flaws, we do not need to hide behind a façade. If we can be honest about our feelings and thoughts, we are stronger than any armor.

Being vulnerable can undermine another's defenses, in a good way. One afternoon during rush hour, I bumped into the back of a sports car entering a highway that flowed like molasses. The driver came out, his face red, his movements aggressive. He walked to my window, and I rolled it down. Before he could speak, I said, "Oh, I am sooo… sorry." He had come prepared for a fight, yet his reactions sputtered as he processed my apology.

Being vulnerable deepens our relationships. At Findhorn we sought to share our feelings with each other. The friendships forged were as strong as steel.

Being vulnerable helped me get over the anxiety I felt when I talked to a group. Stepping into a role or feeling expectations placed upon me was too much pressure. If I pretended to be a good speaker, if I pretended to be knowledgeable, I was haunted by doubts and inevitably made mistakes. By admitting I was nervous, or not an expert, I could then lay that pressure aside and just get on with the talk, enjoying the experience. No pretense. No role to play.

7

The Expansion of Self and the Contractions of Ego

The Ego Gymnastics of Falling In Love

The workshop I signed up for did not start until Monday, so I was left to explore for the weekend. Explore makes it sound like an adventure, but it was not. Many of my new friends went home after the Experience Week. And my roommates spent the weekend shopping in Inverness. Alone in a strange building with strange people, entering the common rooms filled me with a nervous dread. People were laughing and chatting, and I did not belong anywhere. What intuitively felt like home, was empty without people to care about.

I walked into the woods behind Cluny, where my attention was primarily focused on managing my fears. Repeating mantras helped center me: *Others do not give me security, I do ... I am whole within myself ... I do not need others to feel fulfilled.*

Sunday morning I did my laundry. Down there, I met a man from Colorado Springs and told him about my loneliness. He reminded me that others felt the same way, which helped me put my struggle into perspective.

From dreadful aloneness, I swung over to desperately seeking connection, leaning far into others at mealtimes. I knew what I sought did not lie out there, but that did not stop this churning anxiety in my belly. Sunday night my dream reflected this: *I missed the plane to Findhorn.* Certainly, I was missing the point. Being there for me was my goal. Instead I lay in bed fantasizing a partner who understood my spiritual inclinations and would take me under his wing for my safety. Monday morning was a welcome relief.

The workshop was held in the same room as my Experience Week. Eileen Caddy, one of the founders of Findhorn, and François, the current focalizer of the community, led the group. Eileen welcomed us with the caveat, "We thought it would be nice to start on Monday so you could have the weekend to relax." For me, their gift was my nightmare. I was grateful to be part of a group again.

François was a lover of esoteric knowledge. He spoke of themes reminiscent of my studies over the years, adding fresh perspectives and examples. I was so excited. This world was my world. My hidden beliefs could finally emerge into the light of day. This was the answer to my search, a community of like-minded people.

François spoke of the Christ in a new way. The Christ was not Jesus, but a level that many spiritual teachers had reached. They were *christed* beings.

Eileen listed the essentials needed for contacting one's inner voice, an ability she was renowned for. Partly it had to do with intent:

– One must aim for the highest in oneself,

– One should seek healing and purifying experiences to keep one's guidance free of emotional issues or mental distortions,

– One must have faith and act on the directions received,

– One must be grateful.

I absorbed her teachings, but hearing a clear, inner voice seemed far away from my known capabilities.

Next we were led in a guided meditation, to ask our wiser selves how to improve our ability to love unconditionally. These words formed in my mind: *"Release and allow; release from any sort of ties or need for ties. Be in the present and do not form any plans for the future. Be thankful for everything received and everything you can give. And always remember God is within you. You are whole and need not search outside for what you think you lack."*

Eileen mentioned an event that occurred around Christmas, 1967. At that time, there was concern of a nuclear war. The atmosphere was dark; a feeling of doom pervaded people's consciousness. UFO's were considered by Peter and others as a way to escape the planet if a war broke out. But during Christmas of that year, they felt a shift occur that changed everything. Eileen received a message from her inner guide that the love of Christ had been anchored into the earth's etheric plane, one step closer to our material world. The threats dissolved after that.

I remembered this story in particular because of the date. That Christmas, as a teenager, I had mentally ripped myself apart searching for a reason to be here on this planet. Love became my reason to stay. It seemed a surprising parallel.

One very useful talk was given by Michael, a member, who

spoke of the "Perils on the Path." All of them felt like jam pots I could easily fall into. His list included:

1. Projecting a spiritual role, that is build on artifice.

2. Keeping one's head in the clouds, while ignoring who is being walked on.

3. Blaming ourselves for the God gap, the difference between what we aspire towards, and what we are able to do. We must forgive our fallibilities.

4. Judging others on their spiritual paths.

5. Looking outside oneself for our identity and self-worth, and not just for inspiration.

6. Losing faith because of negative thinking; or losing hope because of challenges.

7. Confusing non-attachment with being so detached that one doesn't participate.

8. Pretending sexual feelings are something higher.

9. Thinking that making the right choice is the most important, when in actuality, connecting with our Inner Self is above all else in importance.

10. Staying comfortable and avoiding change; feeling annoyance at those who disturb our complacency.

11. Misunderstanding that the inner call for oneness can be fulfilled by outer actions. The experience of oneness can only be found within.

I loved the workshop. And people commented on how I had changed. I wrote in my diary: *"I've been overwhelmed by compliments here. I am a bit terrified of how big I feel. Joy and energy seem to shine through me. My strength, discipline and power are being seen. How am I so strong when a few days ago I was terrified? As I ride on the crest of expressing myself, I'm afraid of a great fall."*

And my great fall came. I was developing a friendship with Anders, from Sweden. When we first met, in our introductions, I looked into his eyes and recognized his warmth. Getting close would not be difficult. He was easy to be around, open and playful. I careened back and forth between a desire to spend time with Anders and a desire to get to know others.

One day Anders, Laura, a wonderfully grounded Brit from our group, and I walked to the top of a hill behind Cluny, said to be a point of power. We joined hands and meditated. I asked my inner guide if Anders and I would be getting closer. No answer came. Afterwards, we looked silently into each others eyes. His eyes revealed indifference. We would, could, be good friends, and that was all.

A few days later, Maia, my roommate, said Anders hugged her and whispered "I think I'm in love."

She responded, "I bet I know with whom." Both she and Cordula thought I was who he referred to.

Perhaps I had been wrong. Maybe he did feel something for me and was shy about it. So the next day, all warm and loving, I suggested, "Let's spend the night together and see where this goes."

"No, I don't think so," Anders said, "I would not have sex with you here. Maybe if you lived near me in Sweden. I used to hop in bed with anyone, but not lately … I'm surprised you would ask such a thing. You don't display your femininity very much."

My heart sunk. I really had no response to his comments, had nothing to defend myself with. Embarrassed, I went to the sanctuary, to talk with God and clear my confusion. Honestly,

I hadn't thought out my suggestion very clearly. Was I ready to have sex with him or anyone else? No. But he knew exactly what it would mean if we spent the night together. I felt misunderstood, but how else could someone interpret my words. Letting myself feel the cringe of humiliation was painful, yet necessary. How could I face him the next day if I became defensive or hid from the ridiculousness that was me at that moment? *God is my source of love,* was driven home within me. With that knowing, the pain receded.

The next evening we again went up to the power point in silence. At the top of the hill, we smiled at each other from a distance. In the quiet, I asked about a future partner, for I needed some hope at that moment. A quivering feel of expectancy came, as well as a vision of someone who would smile back at me with interest.

Who Anders might have been referring to in his "I think I'm in love" statement was Laura. As I drew away, she and he grew closer. I watched with some envy, seeing how much better suited they were for each other, and struggled with painful weights on my shoulders.

Later, Laura and I talked about Anders. She revealed to me her feelings. "You know, I was envious of you." I laughed and shared my own challenges. We hugged, both of us aware we were caught in a web of painful lessons about relationships.

As the end of the workshop drew near, other group members gave me feedback. Despite all my emotional drifts, from high excitement and joy, to the ripping pain of envy and embarrassment, I was told by someone, "Oh, you're smiling. You must be happy." Another person said, "I don't know why I never got close to you these past 2 weeks. I guess because you're so strong. You don't need me and when weak I don't want to be around someone who is strong."

Those comments hurt. I was ashamed of the powerful energy that expressed through me. We commonly want what we don't have, and for me it was to be delicate and feminine. I was pretty angry at God that night for dealing me such a rough hand. And yet a wiser voice again reminded me, the love and acceptance I sought externally, was really found within. I did not need another's interest to be happy, to feel whole. Faced with what would appropriately be called my ego issues, I knew where fulfillment lay.

THE EGO GYMNASTICS OF FALLING IN LOVE

Our ego, the master of defense in our entourage of character parts, lets go when we fall in love. Hearts open. We have no fear of criticism or judgement. We are filled with happiness.

Unfortunately, the ego's walls always return. If the relationship is worth keeping, we are forced to slog through our defensiveness and try to find our way back to the heaven-like openness we first experienced. To me, this is a meaningful pattern. The blissful first months of a relationship show us what is possible. For the rest, we get the opportunity to grow into someone capable of such pure feelings.

I fell in love with Findhorn during those first weeks. I had found my spiritual home, where my thoughts were understood, my beliefs espoused by others. I felt safe expressing the parts of me mostly hidden. I ran on the juices of joy. I became a powerhouse with all chakras spinning.

But how does one handle all that energy? A novice, I focused my loving energy onto people, and in particular, Anders. I imagined he woke up my love. It was the only way I knew to explain my feelings. If you feel angry, there must be a source. If you love, there must be a person triggering it. I followed my false assumptions unconsciously, and received a brutal wake-up.

Unconscious actions can get one in trouble. Yet we all do it. We must. How do we learn if we don't fumble things and get slammed down by another's reaction? Shame can cause us to bury the event, but facing it forthright adds to our resilience. It hurts. It embarrasses. Our pride is shattered. Yet if we can get through those gritty moments, we can start again. We are a little more humble, a little more aware, and ready for the next bout of ego gymnastics.

8

Encircling and Centering

Negative Self-Talk

It was early spring, and I worked as a long-term guest at Cullerne Gardens, a windswept piece of land that lay between the center of the community and the fishing village of Findhorn. The greenhouses and a large garden area provided some of the food needed for the community kitchens, while the grey stone mansion on the property housed members. As a working guest, I stayed out in the fields, preparing the soil and caring for the few crops that could survive the harsh Scottish winter. My room was in a caravan located in Pineridge, a short walk from the center of the community.

On my first day of work, the March wind was bitingly cold, blowing in from the North Sea. Despite my wool sweater and raincoat, it bore deep into me. After work, I switched on the space heater, and climbed into a hot bath to warm up. The water soothed my muscles, but nothing touched the chill that had reached my bones. I took a hot water bottle to bed, gathering my body around its comforting warmth, and shivered until dawn.

A member named Rory guided our work, an American with Celtic roots, who loved discussing philosophy. A simple question could evolve into a precept for how to live our lives, or a rousing discussion emerge, as we dug into the soil. During breaks, we gathered in one of the sheds around a peat stove, cold fingers encircling hot cups of tea. At the end of each day, we cleaned and oiled our tools, then removed the Wellington boots provided, placing them in a neat row against the wall of the shed.

I often took a shortcut to my caravan through the Gorse-covered sand dunes. The sunlight on the Gorse flowers caused them to exude a scent of coconut, and I inhaled deeply, letting the perfumed warmth relax me after a full day of work. I changed my clothes, then headed to the sanctuary, joining others at the evening meditation. Dinner followed. Entering the Park dining room, I was surrounded by a flurry of activity: children racing around, people connecting with friends, and others filling up their plates from a wide range of dishes.

Over the months working at Cullerne, I shared my caravan with two housemates. Each one challenged me in a different way.

With Daniel, an American, I shared a similar love of esoteric studies. Although in my past I would have leapt at the chance to talk to someone else about a favorite book or concept, over the last months other parts of me were waking up. I wasn't as interested in intellectual discussions, which he seemed to favor.

One night we went to a meeting in the Universal Hall, led by Jay, the new community focalizer. As we walked back towards

Pineridge, Daniel asked, "Do you think he is spiritually evolved enough to be leading the community?" Speechless, my mind filled with questions. Did I think some people were more developed than others? Could we tell the level of a person from a perfunctory examination? I had no way to answer him. My past pattern of analysis and labeling was being replaced by a quiet presence; I could not judge as I had done before.

Once each week, the long-term guests met with David, our focalizer. I looked forward to our meetings. It was a time to take a break, and connect with others who also were staying longer at the community. I took the afternoon bus to Cluny Hill and usually grabbed some tea and a rye cracker slathered in peanut butter and orange marmalade before heading to the small room in a distant wing of the building, where our group met.

We shared how we were doing and often David led us in a guided imagery exercise meant to illuminate our progress. This day was no exception. Eyes closed, we followed his voice into a relaxed state. Then he asked us to connect with our deeper purpose for being in the community. I felt a rise of joy, and shared that with the group.

Daniel repeated his original reason for coming, and included a reference to his readings. Nothing had changed for him. I found myself spacing out, unable to focus on his words. Afterwards, as we travelled back to the Park on the community bus, he asked "What did you think about my sharing? Did it make sense?"

I didn't want to tell him my opinion. What came out spontaneously was an answer I could not have formulated. "I can't feel you in your words. You speak of theories. Where is your heart?" I watched my secreted frustrations travel out on my words, and feared my truth-telling would damage our friendship. He lapsed into silence.

Digging in the soil the next day, I shared my story with Rory. He said, "Hey, you seem rather involved in this. What's up?"

I reflected on the problem, my problem, I recognized. My relationships over the years had been dominated by my analytic brain rather than my heart. The acceptance and safety I found in the community allowed me to soften my grueling intellect, yet I was still very close to being just as mentally-fixated as Daniel seemed to be. He was an example of where I had been and where I did not want to go again. Understanding this, owning my reactions, I was freed to reach out to him in a more open-hearted way.

Another housemate, a Belgium woman named Marie, talked incessantly to me, even through my closed bedroom door. My quiet time was increasingly important, because every day was filled with lessons. I felt a growing tension, as I tried to integrate my experiences, and being interrupted by her chatter only added to my stress. It was rather humorous, being followed around by an eager puppy as I assembled my breakfast in the small kitchen of our caravan. But my patience was stretching thin.

One intense day, I finally said, "Please, I need some quiet."

Marie backed away easily, more resilient than I had given her credit for.

Despite my addressing both roommates as carefully as I could, I feared my words were clumsy and hurt them. My fears rebounded in self-recrimination.

My sister, whom I had called from one of the telephone booths at Cluny, gave me some surprising news. "Phil asked me to marry him," she told me.

My gut tightened. Phil was a nice man, yet I could not think that my sister would be happy bound to him for her lifetime. I feared her entrapment in an unfulfilling marriage, like my mother's. "I don't think it's a good idea, Bu."

Afterwards, gnawing doubt grew in me. *What right do I have to express my opinion on someone else's life? Do I even know what I'm talking about?* It terrified me to speak my truth. Sometimes my inner knowing felt so strong I had to blurt it out. The damage I could do scared me.

I was haunted by this series of interactions. Holding myself together was becoming more and more difficult. One evening, I curled up in a fetal position, overwhelmed by feelings of guilt for the imagined hurts I had inflicted, and shame for the intensity behind the messages I expressed.

I had to find my way back to some semblance of self-forgiveness. There was a healing workshop beginning that weekend, to be held at Drumduan, a large, grey stone house located near Cluny. Desperate for help, I registered the next day. And I had the prescience to ask for my own room. Although they said it was unlikely, I moved from the caravan park into a room of my own at Cluny for a week, a rare commodity.

The path to Drumduan led through a forest, and the quiet walk each morning was a perfect transition from the busy halls of Cluny. The workshop was set in the large living room, a circle of chairs surrounding the ever-present candle in the center. It was led by two community members, one a strong German woman, Uta, skilled in Martial arts, and the other, a gentle, elderly British woman, Barbara, knowledgeable about flower essences.

64

I soaked up their teachings. Ute taught us about centering, standing steadfast in oneself, and not leaning too far back or too far forward. My partner for this exercise pushed my shoulders and, if centered, I could remain standing. If not, I lost my balance. I learned to put my attention into my gut area and hold steady from there.

This very physical experience translated into a method for relating to others. Staying steady in my space, I could handle others' energies without being thrown off. One benefit from the centering exercise was a change in my voice. A side effect of the stress I'd been feeling was the return of the lump in my throat and a voice higher pitched than normal. Centering released that pressure.

Living in a centered way was a new challenge. Over the last few months, I yearned for romance and whenever I met someone I was attracted to, I watched my attention divert from self-focus. Envy, as much as I cringed to admit it, also reared its ugly head. On Friday nights, the community held dances. I loved to dance, and it felt painful watching others flirting and enjoying each other while I sat on the sidelines.

As I held the feel of centeredness, I noticed a contentment arising. Socially I was more relaxed, letting relationships develop in their own timing. I learned to listen to my needs, sitting alone when I needed to, leaving a group when I needed to, not talking unless it felt right. Centering brought me calmness. And the calmer I became, the deeper I connected with others.

A test of my resolve came when Malcolm, a Scotsman and a member at Cluny, sat next to me at lunch. He asked, "How is it going for you?" His brown eyes were warm and inviting.

I was surprised he had sought me out for a conversation.

"Oh, I am pretty much on overload. So many people, so many experiences."

He nodded. "Yeah, it can get really overwhelming."

I continued, "I think my inner is more challenging than anything else. I am so self-critical and doubt myself too much." Feeling free to speak, we talked for quite some time, gazes locked as we shared about our experiences in the community.

Afterwards I reflected on the rush of pleasure moving through me. With my new found centeredness, I was able to stay with myself, knowing all I needed lay within. In the natural scheme of things, we may become friends, or not. And that is not in my control. What is in my control is reminding myself of what is truly important, my relationship with the God within.

While attending the healing workshop, the bedroom I was assigned gave me much needed breathing room. Each evening I spent alone, thinking about my day. My confidence was increasing. Midway through, I received a letter from my best friend, Robin. I was waiting for it, having recently sent her my first letter, describing in glowing terms my experiences of the community. Her response was unexpected, a shock. In it, she accused me of abandoning everyone back in Madison. She said they were deeply hurt by how I left.

I crumpled to the floor, flooded with pain. "I am a shit." Lying in bed that night, my arms encircled my heart and gut, sick with guilt. I was worthless.

The next day I dragged myself to Drumduan, my energy gone. I sat, dimly hearing, and when break time came, slid to the floor. Eyes closed, gripped by emotional pain, I heard a distant voice ask if she could help. Bending over me was Barbara, her eyes soft with concern, concentrating her love upon me. It did not register. *Why is she here when she could be taking a break, having a snack?* She held her wrinkled hands above my heart, radiating healing. Her kindness filled me up and I quietly wept under her gentle care. A universal love came through her and cradled me in its arms.

"You are a silly little girl, thinking you weren't loved," she said.

I smiled, as my energy shifted. It was as if a great rainstorm had washed through me and the sun was shining again. I quickly rose up, strengthened by a knowing of my worthiness.

A seed of hope was planted in me that day, the day I felt unconditional love from Barbara. Before then, I never believed another person would sacrifice their own wants to give me love. I was to take that lesson and apply it in my relationship with my clients, many years later.

After the workshop, I went for a week to the Isle of Erraid, off the west coast of Scotland. A group of community members lived there as caretakers, growing food and keeping watch over the herds of sheep on the rocky land. Erraid is a tidal island, and when our bus arrived, the tide was in and a member rowed over to pick us up. I shared a room in one of a series of stone cottages. They were built in a straight row on the east side of the island, sheltered from the Atlantic Ocean's strong winds by rising hills. The gardens stretched out in front of the row houses, stone walls protecting the plants. The outhouses were in the back yard, requiring a quick run if someone was unlucky enough to need one at night.

I helped with chores in the morning, then put on the proffered Wellington boots to take walks on the soggy peat trails in the afternoon. The wind swept the crests of the hills, and I explored, finding green valleys where the sheep grazed, and carefully climbing the cliffs near the coast, to watch seals resting below me on rocks splashed with ocean spray.

It was a time for spreading myself out, letting my thoughts trail behind in the whipping wind. For months I had grappled with the decision, "Should I become a member or move on?" I was tired of that question. Simplicity was what I yearned for, being with the weeds in the garden, roaming the hills and rocks, and experiencing deep slumber in the cold Scottish nights.

It was in this rarefied atmosphere a dream came: *I was holding a child, an infant born to a friend of mine, to whom I was deeply connected. The baby and I were so close, we questioned whether to keep it with me. As I held it, the baby said, "You must keep me and we should stay in this community."*

The next morning, looking out the small window onto the main drive and gardens beyond, I recognized some new arrivals. It was Hans, whom, with his wife and baby girl, Marina, I had just seen at the community. The symbolism was synchronicity at its best. A new 'me' was growing, still at the baby stage, requiring the nurturance of Findhorn to develop and mature.

After a week, I returned to the main community, electing to stay at Cluny and join the garden crew there, while I prepared for my next steps. The Garden group kept up the grounds, worked a vegetable garden, and maintained an herbaceous border, filled with flowering perennials, that lined the lower walkway.

A membership interview was scheduled with David, my focalizer. When he questioned my motives for joining the community, all I could say was, "I know this is right." I was accepted and prepared to leave, planning to return in the fall to do the Orientation program and become a member.

NEGATIVE SELF-TALK

Every criticism we hear, or repeat to ourself, can stick, if we let it, until we are taken down. For negative thoughts weaken, while positive ones fill a person with strength. I often asked my clients, "Whose voice is saying those words?" It is commonly a parent or teacher's voice speaking in our mind. Like a scratch upon the recording of our memories, the negative ones repeat and repeat. No matter how many times our mother adored things about us, the one correction is what we'll remember. And carry with us in our lives.

There is surely a survival value in remembering the negative comments. They can be seen as course corrections. But for those with a propensity for self-criticism, those negative comments can tear away any semblance of self-love. The repairs required often involve years of reframing, where we substitute positive thoughts for our automatic negative ones.

Sometimes we may need a re-parenting. I think to know one is unconditionally loved is the most healing gift we can be given. Many therapists hold that awareness for their clients, helping them rewrite their negative scripts. Barbara held that awareness for me.

9

Group Consciousness

Inner Guidance in Decision-Making

I was not someone who committed easily. I never stepped further than my toes into the waters of a mediocre future. I had not married; had no desire for children or felt a career calling me. I could not bear to be trapped in a life without meaning, with people who did not see deeper. What convinced me to commit myself to this mystery school called Findhorn was this very honest admission by Charlie during my Experience Week. "You're going to want to look up to the members, expect more from us. But remember we are the same as you, trying for something better, but often failing. Keeping focused on our spiritual nature while facing our problems is what keeps us moving forward."

Just off the train in the late October morning, I greeted Jon, the driver of the community bus come to pick up travelers. *I'm home.* A happy warmth spread through me. Of course, home was at my mother's house, where I was always welcome. Findhorn held a different meaning; a spiritual one.

While here, I would be free from the loving, but at times critical, pushing and pulling that described my family relationships. During my time as a guest I had unnecessarily carried on that family tradition in an environment where few judged or had an agenda for me. I was finding as my resilience grew, others' opinions meant less, and friends' heartfelt feedback meant much more. I hoped the community would be a safe place to nurture my more sensitive side, a side that needed, and desperately wanted, to express itself in the world.

My start would begin with Orientation, a seven-week program preparing new members to step out into the community. At Park Reception, I was directed to one of the four cedar bungalows surrounding a meditation garden in the center of the community. This would be my living quarters for the next three weeks. My housemates had already arrived: Cor, a smiling, handsome man from Holland; Ian, a sweet, shy Englishman; and Katharina, already a good friend from my time at Cullerne.

I adored Katharina. Coming from Germany, she barely spoke English when she arrived, yet her broad smile lit up a room. Our friendship would deepen during Orientation. We supported each other as we adapted to the community. I was to find over my five years at Findhorn that Katharina's generous heart, so apparent at first, was matched by her capacity to wield truth. She was always seeking to find the lesson behind an experience and had a killer instinct for ferreting out what was really going on with someone.

That afternoon, our Orientation focalizers, Gordon and

Sophia, gave us an in-depth tour of the Park, ending with an invitation to tea by different community members. It was a lovely way to spend my first day back.

Afterwards, we re-grouped in the Park Building. Sitting in front of a crackling fire, I warmed my hands while we shared our stories.

Then Sophia led us in a purpose meditation. *What was our reason for being here?* A question repeated multiple times during my stay, it always revealed a slightly different answer. Like peeling the layers of an onion, each was meaningful in the moment; each took me a little deeper into myself.

I received the words, *"Openness... You must learn to stay open."* Whew! The wisdom from my inner guide always surprised me. How quickly I allowed my mind to lead, organizing and labelling members of the group, when it was my heart that should be greeting them. I decided to keep *Openness* as my mantra for the duration.

The Park Garden was my choice as a work department for the next three weeks. The crew maintained the original garden, the one Peter started lettuce and radishes in twenty-two years before. The patch of ground expanded, assisted by hundreds of visitors and eventual members of the burgeoning community. The land had been windswept sand dunes, and was now an oasis of life.

One of the rituals I loved as a guest was the time set aside for personal sharing before we began our work. Around the circle, we spoke of our present journey, then joined hands, closed our eyes and attuned to the moment and to the people we were with.

To my surprise, the Park Garden focalizer did not make time

for sharing. Evidently, many of the older members arrived before the educational programs began, and they focused more on work and less on getting to know everyone a little better. I told my housemates of my disappointment. Ian, who planned to join the Park Garden Department when a member, determined to reinstate the practice.

Early one morning I walked down a broad tunnel of beech hedging. A whoosh sounded behind me and I stepped aside. Three swans sailed past in a perfect v-formation. Their only sound was the rhythmic humming of their wings. In unison, they gently lifted higher to cross over the fields, heading south. The symmetry of their flight was a foretelling of what would follow for me. This morning I would take part in a workshop on Group Consciousness.

Our group gathered in the weaving studio. We sat cross-legged on a colorful carpet, surrounded by textiles and yarns, craft tables and a large loom. A member spoke to us about working together as a group. The consciousness that exists in each being, also exists on a group level. He led us in an exercise to experience that consciousness.

In the center of the circle, six members, including myself, were tasked with deciding on a group purpose while the larger membership watched. Given a limited time period to achieve our goal, we first approached the issue rationally by talking it out. Each of us gave our opinion of a good group purpose.

Mariana tried to slip out of stating her view. "I'll go along with what everyone else decides."

"No. We all must contribute equally," Terry said.

At the end, every member had a different take, showing us just how divided we were.

Next we decided to get guidance by asking within. As we emerged from our light trance, Karl, one of the members, said "I don't think we have enough time for the whole group to share our insights."

He looked towards Jessica, who was known to have psychic abilities. "What did you get?" he asked, as if her guidance would be better than the others.

I watched in shock, as Karl, with good intentions, took control of the group. My blood began to simmer. This hierarchical way of leadership was one reason I had opted out of the regular work world. "Wait a minute. That's not right," I said. "Everyone should share or what was the point of attuning."

We agreed to stick to our original plan, and heard from each person. Funnily enough, Jessica had nothing. Only myself and Andre had gotten messages, and they were similar. The lesson I took from this was profound. The group's guidance dwelt in the pool of minds, not in a particular person. There may be a leader (or focalizer), but the wisdom rested in the group and could be brought to the light of day by any member. Giving everyone a chance to speak took longer, but was time well spent.

Another lesson was equally important. The most effective outcome is when each member feels empowered enough to speak out. If certain members just go along with the others, the decision loses its potency.

One aspect of group consciousness was played out in the community's consensual decision-making. Often a decision did not need a community-wide vote. Yet when the members were deciding to buy the land their buildings were on, including the money-making caravan park, they met as a whole. It took about three days to air the fears, concerns and hopes of every member, until none were left unspoken. Then all two hundred and fifty people went into meditation and asked for the best way forward. The answer they got was clear: buy the park. The fund raising, after this decision, was smooth and easy. Eileen received the guidance that they would buy the land with thousands of small donations from all over the world. And that is exactly how the money came in. The power of a group all focused on the same goal was formidable.

Another aspect of group consciousness, a rather 'magical' one, occurred towards the end of my time as a guest. Piles of earth appeared around the steps leading down to the garden at Cluny. I asked Pieter, Cluny's focalizer, what was happening.

"The sewer is clogged," he said. "We've been digging to find the blockage, but so far, nothing. It's been a few weeks and I'm ready to call a meeting of all the members to look at what might be blocking us ... you know, maybe spiritually, or psychologically."

My curiosity was piqued. "Please can I be a part of that meeting? I promise to stay quiet in the back of the room. I just want to know how the Cluny membership works together. I'm gonna be a member myself pretty soon."

Pieter agreed, and when I walked into the room, he directed me to sit on the floor in the back. Then he called the meeting to order. "We have not found the sewer's blockage. It's time for us to look deeper into why. Is there something that needs to be aired, some stuckness?"

A few members, one by one, spoke of certain problems they were having with Pieter, in particular. He had not included them in many of his decisions. Others felt the expertise in their department was not valued, that he ought to let them help more. Unaware of the part he played in the blockage, to his credit Pieter was able to hear their feedback. He promised to listen to and include others more in the day-to-day running of the place. A lightness filled the room and the meeting ended with humor and good will. The next day the sewer cleared.

INNER GUIDANCE IN DECISION-MAKING

At the community, many group decisions are made by asking within. Inner guidance is less of a skill and more a willingness to lay aside one's personal wants and ask what would be best for all. It is believed a fount of wisdom exists that we can tap into by asking our question then listening within. The guidance may source from our higher self, or from another spiritual being. Some of us receive an answer in meditation, some in dreams, some hear words, or see images. Some feel a physical sensation. At times no answer comes, and we realize, as I did back in Chicago when deciding to leave, that using our free will is just as important in certain situations as following our inner guidance.

Not everyone is able to receive words or images. Peter had a strong intuitive sense, but followed the guidance of Eileen and Dorothy religiously. Eileen was asked to check within for even the most mundane of questions, such as which company to order the linens from. For Peter, the greater good was included in even the smallest of decisions.

Seeing this process applied to group decision-making astonished me, because it worked. Asking within, we laid our differences aside. And we could be confident that the answer we reached was best for all.

10

Opening Pandora's Box

Taking Back One's Projections

The term openness was a constant companion during my time in Orientation. Yet that quality brought me troubles as well as joys. Emotional wounds emerged to be healed; hopes rose up, desiring to be fulfilled. My ego suffered the consequences; while my soul reaped nuggets of truth.

I dreamed *a girlfriend was wounded, with sores spread over her body. On her left foot was a gaping hole. A translucent worm poked its head out, then hid back inside. Finally it emerged, becoming a long snake. It slithered into the pool next to us, invisible in the waters. I worried for those in the pool, yet was grateful my friend had been freed.*

The next evening, William offered me a foot massage. William was an older Brit, who had entered Orientation with his girlfriend, Jessica. Smooth and charming, his magnetic personality and good humor were hard to resist. As he worked on my right foot, I endured the painful pinches between my toes, knowing it would be followed by a pleasurable flow of tingling warmth when he was done. My left foot reacted more sensitively to his touch and my body weakened. Uncomfortable memories flowed by: old emotions from conflicts I had with a roommate in Madison, feelings of insecurity and the pain of dulling depressed states. After the massage, I lay quietly for some time, allowing myself to release those memories slowly.

I loved my new group. There were twenty-two of us to get to know. However, the more my heart opened, the more susceptible I was to fantasies of romance and ill-advised desires.

The last evening we spent at the Park, we had a party with music. A favorite song of mine played, full of swelling rhythms. I asked if anyone wanted to dance. William stood up and we spun around the cleared floor, totally in sync, the group watching and clapping. Breathless afterwards, we laughed and hugged.

That night I dreamed *William and I were getting closer and closer. We were on the edge of consummating a relationship. But I was aware of Jessica, his previous girlfriend. Her jealousy and feelings of anger were reflected in her scarred and bruised face, an image that haunted me. "I can't do this, William. Look at her. She is suffering so much." He pulled me closer, saying, "She's alright. It's okay." I kissed him then, but my feelings were still conflicted.*

Thus began a time of love and pain. My dreams continued to warn me to be cautious. *I found my sister lying limp in someone's arms. She had been bitten by a white shark, a very pretty little fish, but it had sucked the life force out of her. She would survive, but was unconscious for the moment.* Even after this dream, my feelings rushed forward, blinded by desire.

We travelled to Erraid for the week. It was common for the

Orientation groups to schedule a visit to the west coast isle. The wildness of the Atlantic and the harsh conditions the Erraid members endured, contrasted sharply with the temperate life at Findhorn. The bus dropped us off at the end of the road, just across from the tidal island. The waters had receded so we gathered our luggage and trekked across the bay.

After my dream, I made efforts to avoid William, fruitless as they were. We were given a tour, and then I quietly pulled away to walk along the coastline. Standing on the shore, the sounds of the lapping water settle me after the long drive. When I looked up, there was William, also looking out over the water. We smiled across the distance. My feelings were growing, unexpressed but powerful. I felt pulled, in a fever of sorts, towards him.

That first evening, we met as a group to share, followed by appreciations. William flooded me with his loving appraisal and I could only return it by appreciating him. I was also grateful for Gordon, who as our focalizer was present fully, a warm, caring man who saw us as real people rather than as orientees. Gordon shared his heart with us, as well as his years of experience at the community.

One evening he told us the unfiltered history of Findhorn. His story illustrated both the lighter and the darker aspects of the community, the fantastic and the delusional, the successes and the failures. Gordon kept his feet on the ground and helped us do so as well.

This evening, after all the appreciations, my heart felt as if it would burst with the love I received.

The next day we caught a ferry to visit the isle of Iona. Iona was the home for a monastic order founded by St. Columba.

The remains of their grey stone abbey still stood, and drew tourists. Many visitors travel there for a spiritual retreat.

The isle is a small one with only one road extending the length. I walked down it with William, Jessica and Katharina. Despite his words last night and my hopes that William and I would grow closer, he was distant. No questions for me about my life, no interest in who I was. When I tried to ask about him, he danced around anything personal. True to his Piscean nature, he floated away from being pinned down. The warmth from my heart shifted to a more heated frustration.

William had informed the group earlier that he and Jessica had an open relationship. So it wasn't shocking when I entered the kitchen to help clean up dinner dishes, and spotted him and Katharina in a passionate embrace. I backed out quickly. At first a sickening pain filled my gut, which quickly reverted to revulsion. I buried my jealousy under rationalizations: *he is not worth caring about; he is a shameless flirt, a player.*

I went to the evening discussion group, but could not be present. My heart had slammed shut. So I left early. Passing a bookshelf on my way to bed, a title called out to me: *The Wounded Woman – Healing the Father-Daughter Relationship.*

All night and the next morning, while hidden in a cave of blankets, I read the book cover to cover, and realized my projections. Some of William's traits reminded me of my father, a soft and dreamy elusiveness that disappoints. I cried for my father, for the pain held in our family.

And Gordon reminded me of my brother. Both of them were solid, beefy men with a sensitive, caring nature. I cried for my brother, who tried to take responsibility for us after my father left; who had a warm-hearted protectiveness as the elder brother, despite his use of force to get us to cooperate.

Not usually demonstrative, a few evenings before, I had impulsively come up from behind Gordon and hugged him. He laughed, receiving my affection without any complicated calculations. Perhaps my feelings towards him emerged more easily because of my love for my brother.

After a day of facing myself, I understood my projections upon William and Gordon were more about my own family dynamics. Pulling Gordon aside, I cleared the air. "You remind me of my brother and I may have projected on you a bit, for which I'm sorry." Sharing my insights was empowering, and received well by Gordon. Yet revealing myself to William would take me more time. The work with my inner father was just beginning.

When we returned to the community, settling into Cluny this time, I shared a room with Morley, a bright, outspoken Australian. Having a strong personality, she hooted and howled when energized, giving me the opportunity to be as uncouth and outspoken as I wanted. We supported each other and grew a deep friendship.

I told her of my feelings towards William. Her view was novel. "I think he's a bit of a scammer, pretending to be all loving but I'm not sure he really is."

One dream summarized my confusion about my father and William. *I was going to another house my father owned, but we could not get it together to make the train on time. We fumbled about. I noticed my father had a face on both sides of his head.*

I tried to ignore William, which felt wrong in so many ways. I don't tolerate indifference easily, mine or another's, and we had been so warm and friendly previously. I finally asked to meet for a talk in the small sitting room upstairs.

I started. "I don't know if you have noticed, but I am pretty shut down to you. Feelings around my father have been coming up, and you remind me of him, and that makes it harder to relate to you."

"I haven't noticed anything," he said. He held himself back, did not seem to want to discuss my issue.

It wasn't easy for me to lay my problems onto his smooth, unruffled surface. I hoped to hear *What can we do to shift things for you? I'd like us to be friends.* I hoped for us to emerge from this talk feeling a bit closer, but William was well-defended.

"Others have said the same thing, that I remind them of their father," he continued.

I thought to leave it at that point, but nothing was resolved inside me, so I shifted my tactic. "Why do you seem so emotionless?"

He stiffened. "I aim for detached affection."

Something you got from The Course in Miracles, I thought, as he had previously been a teacher of those books. I couldn't resist saying, "You seem more detached than affectionate."

"Probably true," he returned.

I began again. "I'm not comfortable with how our relationship is. It's superficial, jokey, lacks depth. Although that is true for many people I know, we had gotten along so well, previously. I hoped we could go deeper." He didn't respond, his marbled edifice staying strong.

"You are supposed to love me!" I blurted out, thinking of the importance of love on the spiritual path. But probably I was speaking more to my father than to him at this point. This is the line I would regret the most.

His cold demeanor grew. "I generally don't do what others tell me I am supposed to."

My frustration blew up and I dived for the throat. "At times you don't feel human to me!"

"Others have said that about me," he responded cooly.

The pit bull in me came out, faced with his continuous deflection of my statements and his unwillingness to relate to me. "You are philosophically arrogant!" I accused.

Something shifted in William then. He took a deep breath, closed his eyes and began speaking. "I see fear in your eyes and that fear would prevent my relating to you. I also see expectation and that has kept me away from you. I noticed you were very mental, and I don't need more mentality, so I've not been interested in getting to know you." He said he was drawn to Katharina because of her open heart.

As the words sunk in, I felt cut to the quick, and began weeping.

"I wonder where that came from?" he pondered, as if they weren't his words but came from a deeper source. Then he sat 'compassionately' and watched while I cried.

Minutes later, I was ready to end. "Thank you for what you said. It was honest and to the point."

I left feeling complete and slowly walked to the Beechtree Room. We were meeting with Bert, a long time member, to talk about our psychological and spiritual development. Torn apart by William's words, yet remarkably calm, I faced the truth: I was seen as a fearful, expectant and very wrong person. I kept a wide distance from him in the circle.

Bert had a sweet kindness about him. He was relaxed and shared his perspectives and humor easily. He spoke about the stressors new members face and the spiritual journey one takes as a member.

During his talk, William asked why it was necessary to have so many psychological and emotive workshops in the community.

"Aren't we here for spiritual growth rather than therapy?" he asked.

Bert replied, "My spiritual growth is on learning to love and that entails dealing with all parts of my being, including my emotional self. Emotions are to be acknowledged and worked on, which is especially important for the men of this community."

William began to ask another question. "If one's spiritual work is done in the work departments then why ..."

He was interrupted by a number of the group who knew where he was headed, "No William, spiritual work involves every part of one's life," they said in unison.

Taken aback by the group's response, he spoke out, "Am I going to have to defend myself from more people wanting to talk to me?"

The tension towards William was palpable. He had entered Orientation so open and affectionate, but over the weeks had pulled back into a very cool, rational and seemingly heartless stance. The group, as a whole, recognized William's refusal to share and relate meaningfully. I could see the part I played as a cutting edge of that tension. My small purposes were part of a larger stream of pressure to get William to open his heart.

In my family, I missed an acknowledgement of who I was or the unique gifts I possessed. This yearning, this empty spot inside me, was what I met William with. He had singled me out in the beginning, only to pull away when I wanted more. Like the danger of opening Pandora's box, his initial flirting released desires and wants in me, and triggered this drama which brought so much insight. I was grateful, but also regretted having imposed on him. Just as the snake in my dream had left my girlfriend's foot only to threaten others in the pool, working on the pain I felt about my father threatened those around me, in particular William. But he was not wholly innocent. There was a lesson there for him, if he wanted to grasp it.

Our relationship improved over the next days. My pain receded as I learned to not look for something more than he could give. We laughed and stayed on the surface and after Orientation he disappeared from my awareness, moving into other parts of the community.

Yet how to handle the love energies coursing through me? One evening, Roger came in to talk about emotions. I had to ask, "How do you handle feelings of love when they are so strong you might just explode?" He suggested, "Do something physical. Work in the garden as a way to ground the energy." Clearly a better option than grounding the energy in another person.

TAKING BACK ONE'S PROJECTIONS

Projection is one of the more common defensive strategies described in psychology. Unwanted feelings are displaced onto another person.

For example, when an individual is threatened by his own angry feelings, he may ascribe angry motives to others.

The process of projecting is a part of everyday living as well. A stranger may look similar, or feel similar to a member of our family. Our mind is busy linking our past relationships to the person in front of us. Partner's traits often reflect one of our parents. We might project onto others our dreams and desires, as parents often do with their children. Friends may display qualities we would like for ourselves.

Most projections are harmless and the projector can be woken up with a little effort. For example, the grown child can say, "I don't want to be a doctor," shattering his parents' projected dream, the one they wished they could have fulfilled themselves.

Taking back our projections is an important tool in self work. Whenever we are critical of someone or unreasonably upset about something they did, we are likely projecting onto them our own issues. At the community, when I judged or felt negative towards someone, I often asked myself, "Who do they remind me of? Are my feelings towards my mother seeping out into how I feel about this person?"

And I looked within whenever I caught myself thinking critically about another. If someone's arrogance bothered me, I asked myself, "Where is my arrogance?" It was not hard to find my own version. Then the tension between us more easily dissipated. Every trait I noticed in another, I found in myself, to a greater or lesser degree. Acknowledging its presence returned my focus back to where it belonged, on my own issues.

11

The Angel of Adventure

Making Mistakes

The piercing January winds blew outside the window of Cluny's common room, as my Orientation Group gathered around the blazing hearth. The brightly lit space was filled with the sounds of moving chairs, chatting people, and crackling embers.

It was our final meeting. Excitement for the future filled me, but there were also remnants of sadness. Another ending. The more endings I experienced, the easier they became. But that's not to say they weren't sad for me. I was learning to accept loss and the shifts my friendships took. One would not survive at Findhorn if constancy rather than change was a top priority.

One area that remained fairly stable was the structured work days. Becoming a member meant joining the work department one attuned to. We would also take on the responsibilities that came with membership. No matter our job, we would be teachers, sharing our growth lessons with each other and sharing our perspectives of community life with the guests. I felt more than ready to make that transition. Many of my closest friends were here in this circle, starting out just as I. We would likely help each other on this journey.

Our first order of business was to finalize jobs. New members usually start out doing support work: cooking, dining room, gardening, housekeeping, and maintenance. Theresa, the focalizer of Cluny Garden, seemed very happy to welcome me to her crew. When I asked in meditation whether working in the garden was the right choice, my heart lit up. Others in our group had found their jobs in a similar way.

Our last act was to draw an Angel Card to help with our next step. The cards were spread out in the center of our circle, face down. We silently asked for the best quality to carry with us as we stepped into the community. I reached for the brightest one, likely brightest only to me as the light reflected differently depending on where you sat. I held it in my hand for a few seconds, then turned it over. It was a picture of an angel stepping forward, walking stick in hand, wearing a backpack. The word ADVENTURE was printed in big letters next to it.

Adventure! A whoosh of panic lifted me up and I rushed out of the room. Finding my way to the outside, I stood on the threshold and looked out over the hillside. The fresh air took my mind off the overwhelming pressure of that word, a momentary break from the confused thoughts filling my brain.

Life as an adventure....terrifying!

A flood of memories passed though my mind: the mistakes, the pain of loneliness, the self-criticisms, the failures that haunted me my first year. My eyes teared up.

Stepping forward consciously, with an adventurous spirit, is not what I do. Could I even manage the courage for this next step, much less face the future smiling? I was standing on a precipice, unsure and afraid. Sitting down on the step, my hands pressed against the concrete, as if I needed to push against something solid.

Gordon opened the door behind me and stepped out to find a seat. "Hey, are you okay?"

"I'm fine," I assured him, wiping away some lingering trails of wetness on my cheeks. He glanced at my card. Even saying the word "ADVENTURE" sent my stomach churning. I couldn't capture my overwhelm at getting that card. I stumbled over my words, trying to find the right ones, and only succeeded in mashing my thoughts up.

Aware that the others were waiting, I pulled out of myself with a slight laugh. "Whew, what a powerful reaction!" We rose and I followed him back to the meeting room.

The others were sharing about their angels. When my turn came, all I could say was, "My angel is ADVENTURE. I don't know why it freaks me out, but it does. Life as an adventure seems too much."

Orientation ended with Sophia and Gordon releasing us. The next day, the ties of our group loosened, as my friends scattered around the community. Some moved to the Park to be nearer their jobs, and many of us stayed at Cluny. Gordon and Sophia returned to their homes in the Park and prepared for their next steps. Both chose to leave the community soon after our group finished. The Orientation program appeared to be the beginning for us, and the beginning of the end for them.

I was excited to get a room of my own, after a year of sharing with others. The room was one of five off a long hallway in the back of the building. Previously, these were used as staff quarters for the hotel. Peter, Eileen and Dorothy had made it a priority to fix up the rooms, brightening them with paint and flowers to show their appreciation to their staff. It was one of many changes they made when they took over management.

A tiny room, but I was grateful for any space to call my own. Sheets and blankets were left for me to put on. I lined the top of the bureau and windowsill with my collection of pictures, scarves, stones and mossy branches. My books were in a pile on the desk. Finally my backpack could be emptied and my clothes put in drawers.

I joined the Cluny Garden group on Monday. Theresa and Peggy were the only members, but slowly our group would grow as the weather warmed. By summer we would be six women.

Our first meeting was in the Sanctuary. The two welcomed me into the garden department, imagining me entering their circle. A quiet joy filled me. *This is where I belong.* Afterwards, we collected our teas and met in a small room overlooking the garden to get to know each other.

Theresa was an American with French roots. She held her authority delicately, her strength shifting like the branches of a rowan in a soft breeze. Intelligent and sensitive, she understood the challenges of starting out. As a tender new member, I needed their support, and she gathered me under her wing, protecting me as I grew.

Peggy was a Canadian, who had joined the community a year before me. Possessing a gentle kindness, she was very accepting, but did not leave to chance someone having a distorted view. She squirmed uncomfortably as she spoke her truth, so sensitive was she to how it might impact the other person. Yet this was why we were here, to get honest feedback and grow consciously. Our friendship was forged over our time in the garden.

Cluny Garden included all the land around the building, which was situated on the side of Cluny Hill. Below was a lovely wooded lawn with a small tinkling spring and a perennial border that supplied flowers for the workshops and dining room. Near the maintenance shed in the back was a greenhouse and below was the vegetable garden which supplied some of the vegetables needed for the kitchen. A high beech hedge outlined the property.

It was the middle of winter in northern Scotland and my wool sweaters and windbreaker were essential for gardening. At the start of the work day, we met inside the warm greenhouse. On the right were rows of tiny plants soaking up the light from the south-facing windows, moisture drops collecting on the glass. In one corner was a peat-burning stove. Lined up near the doorway was a collection of black Wellington boots.

We shared our names (as there were usually a small number of new guests each week who joined us) and how we were doing. Then we held hands and quietly attuned. Finally, we grabbed a pair of boots, filled our wheelbarrows with tools and went out to work.

When offered to focalize the vegetable garden, I jumped at the chance. I was eminently practical and putting my efforts into food growing inspired me far more than growing flowers. As I look back, being the vegetable gardener was a task way beyond my capacity. I wonder whether much actually made it up to the kitchen during my watch. Luckily the kitchen ordered most of their vegetables from a distributor. A productive garden was not the highest on my list of priorities then. My first priority was myself, and being in the garden grew me. A job at Findhorn was never just a job, it was a path of growth, a journey for the soul.

I began by claiming the garden space. My first act was to build a wild area in a corner, meant to be untouched by humans. ROC had been told to set aside space near each garden for the nature spirits to call their own.

There were foxgloves growing in the corner. A guest, walking through the gardens, mentioned they were poisonous, so I replaced them with other perennial flowers. Stones curving sinuously toward the hedges on each side outlined the corner patch. What I had created was beautiful, and I invited Theresa to check it out. The first thing she noticed while looking at the wild garden was the absence of the foxgloves.

"What happened to them?" she asked.

"I heard they were poisonous so took them out," I said, unaware of any problem.

She raised her brown eyes sadly. "Oh no. They were so beautiful."

Theresa's grief at the loss of those flowers tore at my heart, and I feared she would take the garden away from me. A great need was behind my wanting to have this garden. Throughout my life, I've always wanted a garden of my own, a canvas for me to create upon, unchallenged by anyone else's vision. *The Secret Garden,* where the heroine asked for "a bit of earth" of her own, was a favorite book of mine as a child.

My mistake was a human failing, thinking poisonous meant bad. I had never seen foxgloves before, never knew that they were actually desired in gardens. My self-critic reared up after seeing the disappointment in Theresa's eyes, but she never blamed me. Unlike my family at home, I never experienced criticism from another person in the community. I was to find that every slash to my self-worth was self-administered. The adventure I was on was less external and more a pathway of compassion towards myself.

MAKING MISTAKES

There will be so many times when we make the wrong decision. One can limp away, devastated. Or look within and learn from it. Even committing a very painful mistake can be soothed by kindness to oneself. Reminders such as 'we all make mistakes,' 'there is always tomorrow,' 'nobody is perfect,' and 'mistakes make us stronger' can help when our insides scream. They give us perspective, a distance from the punishing part of us that never lets up. Only when our self-love grows beyond our ego limits can we make mistakes with more ease and maybe with some joy. We are always learning and mistakes are a great way to get further along.

12

The Ups and Downs of Self

Know Thyself

"Our deepest fear is not that we are inadequate. Our deepest fear is that we are powerful beyond measure. It is our light, not our darkness, that frightens us most." Marianne Williamson from *A Return to Love: Reflections on the Principles of "A Course in Miracles"*

The unveiling of my light was a cautious and bumpy process, a journey that required healing many of the old wounds still clinging to me. I revealed my self slowly.

While still a guest, I asked Carol, a member, for a psychic reading. I knew very little of how she worked, but hoped to gain a better understanding of myself. The reading turned out to be a revelation.

We sat in Carol's caravan in the Park. Red curtains covered the daylight, creating a womb-like ambience. She began with her eyes closed, describing her first impressions of me.

"I am seeing a shyness, like you are a little girl of seven peeping from behind screens. One can see you through them but not clearly. Behind the screens are all these qualities: a joyful cheeriness of spirit and a capacity for organization and for guiding others, that would cause people to gravitate towards you. You are a sensitive and lively soul yet your expression is complicated by your insecurities and shyness. You hold up screens to keep all those qualities hidden, allowing them full expression only occasionally."

"It's like you are saying, 'You can have a little of me depending on how safe I feel letting you in. But the me that is really there, I'm saving. I'm afraid of showing it to you. I can't take the risk of exploring what I could really give.' It feels like that would make you lonely, isolated and maybe a bit arrogant."

She continued, "You tell yourself, 'I don't want to stand out,' despite the inner frustration you feel and your lack of fulfillment. There is a fear that maybe your gifts wouldn't be special at all or interesting to others. You are in a very stuck place right now."

Carol looked deeper to find the source of my screens. She saw my childhood as loving but also a training in repression and mediocrity. "Your parents had a low estimation of their own identity. You inherited a sense of insecure self-worth from your mother and particularly from your father. It's almost as if you were too lively as a baby. To them, life had been a struggle and you came in, saying 'You don't have to do that. Here I am already joyful, cheery and full of energy.'"

After the reading, I curled into a corner of Cluny's healing room, and recorded Carol's words into my diary, words I knew to be true. The spirit I had brought into this life was slowly hidden and buried, until by the age of thirty my life's course looked more like a dead end. Luckily, my grandfather's money allowed me to seek something better. This vision quest was the only way I could imagine getting the help I needed.

While reflecting on my parents, memories came up. I was six and sitting on a hill beside the roadway. Whenever a car went by, I smiled and waved. Usually they waved back. Later that night, my father said, "Don't do that. People don't like kids waving at them." It felt as though a bucket of cold water had been dumped on me. Although it was hard to believe all those people did not like to wave hi, I stopped.

And my mother never really understood the inner impulses that moved me. She loved blindly, and showed me an unquestioning life. So much of me felt unseen around her.

Sitting on the floor, I sobbed, those gut sobs that touch so deep. Seeing the contrast between my parents' messaging and my own inner self was a major awakening. As I grieved the loss of my inner child's enthusiasm, I could also see the gift: the damping down of my self was important for my growth, providing me enough discontent to be willing to fight for my freeing. It also protected an innocent me from the painful reactions of a less loving world.

But, in regard to my parents, all I felt was anger. "What the hell?" I exclaimed to the empty room, even though the walls were as innocent as my parents were. They had tried their best, I supposed. But being angry was a necessary first step.

My work lay ahead, and I knew the chains of insecurity would not be easily broken. Integrating all those parts of me would take time. Eventually I'd crawl out from my protective screens, a scary thought at that moment. But I recognized the benefit of being at the community. I could be more of myself here in this safe haven.

A year later, my struggle with self-criticism was still a problem. There is a card in the Thoth Tarot deck that perfectly depicts this: nine swords all pointing downward with blood dripping off their blades. It symbolizes the damage we do to ourselves by thinking negatively. I arrived in the community wounded, having stabbed myself repeatedly. And I was challenged by a fascinating but distressing psychological pattern during my first years, the ups and downs of my self-worth.

Like a pendulum that is held in one position and then released, I had been held by my constraining thoughts, my shyness, and my fears. Letting go allowed expression of all the power, excitement and joy built up inside me. When I showed more profound and exalted parts of myself, I felt bigger, better, and more powerful than others. I might ride on that high for a few hours or days and then crash to the ground when some experience pointed out one of my flaws. I was less than others then, horribly imperfect.

The pendulum of my self-worth swung back and forth. I didn't want to be arrogant. I wanted to see myself as equal to others. And of course I was, but it took me a while to get there. My cycling thoughts between grandiosity and low self-worth reflected a deep insecurity. Eventually they evened out. I would leave the community knowing of my value and that of each one of us.

Later, when I studied Jung for my master's degree, I came across the very same concept, which he called "the inflation and deflation of the ego". The term *ego* referred to the mental construct we have of ourselves – the words we use to describe who we are. Getting to the point where I stopped labeling and comparing myself to another took the better part of two years in the community.

One summer day, I bumped into another member while carrying an armload of vegetables destined for the kitchen.

"Oh sorry. I am such an idiot."

"That's okay. But an idiot you are not. You are being too negative towards yourself," she responded.

More than once, during my time as a guest, I had been told, "You are so hard on yourself." It had surprised me at the time, for I didn't realize how my words were coming across to others. I suspected my self-critiquing was likely a preemptive strike. If I was hard on me, then others wouldn't be.

This time I reflected on her comment for a second. "Yeah, you're right… It's weird. I don't really think of myself as an idiot."

Later, I thought more about it. My confidence had been growing and compassion rather than criticism led the way. I was happy with who I was becoming on the inside. Yet my automatic responses said otherwise. There was a disconnect. From then on I watched my words more carefully. But what was also apparent was how tenuous the strands of change are; and how important it was to protect my budding self-worth.

By winter, a new confidence was peeping out. One evening we community members met in the Universal Hall for a meeting. Two hundred filled the tiers of cushioned benches outlining three sides of the five-sided hall, as if those on the central wooden floor were held in our symbolic arms.

That night it was Jay, Charlie and Noah being held. Jay, the community focalizer, was preparing to step down and announced that both Charlie and Noah were interested in the position.

Charlie had been with the community for years and years. He had spoken during my experience week, winning my admiration by his acknowledgement of his flaws, but I knew little about him as he lived in the Park area. Noah was a long term member and had lived in Cluny ever since I had been there. I often saw him in the halls wearing a distracted, worried look as he raced to get some job done. When he turned his focus onto a person, his friendly smile softened all his features.

Each told of their vision for the community and what prompted them to step up. Charlie was particularly self-effacing, willing to support Noah having the position if he was not wanted.

As with all major decisions, it was never about who we liked better. It had more to do with who was the 'right' choice, the one who was supposed to be there. We left the meeting, letting the question rest within to see what emerged. Core group and the board members of the Findhorn Foundation would ultimately decide the next focalizer, for they had the responsibility for the practical running of the place.

That night I tried to sleep but couldn't. A powerful knowing was growing inside me and I had to sit down and write to Charlie. I told him what I saw as he spoke. It felt like he was backing into that position of greater responsibility, fearful and reluctant to take on the mantle. It was a fear that likely sourced from his relationship with Peter. Peter had ruled with the qualities of a boss, which I imagined Charlie was fearful of recreating. I saw him as our next focalizer, but he would have to be willing to step up and face the challenge of leadership squarely.

The force that kept me up dissipated after I got all my thoughts on paper and I quickly fell asleep. The next morning the letter was sent off and I continued with my day.

A week later, I had heard nothing from Charlie, so thought no more about it. Then one lunchtime I was sitting at a table of friends when Giles, one of the Foundation's board members, approached. "Is it okay to sit here?" "Sure." I tried to hide my shock. *What does he want?* I had never talked to him before and as far as I was concerned he was many steps above me in the hierarchy of my imagination.

"I wanted to meet you. I was at the board meeting and Charlie read your letter to us. I wanted to meet the person who wrote that letter." I was speechless. I felt a nobody and here Giles was telling me what I had done actually mattered.

That evening I thought about the small light from my soul that found its way onto that paper, and knew I was closer to expressing my true Self.

KNOW THYSELF

Know Thyself is the most known of three Greek maxims over the entrance to the temple at Delphi. I first came across the phrase while reading Plato. Socrates taught his students to look within above all else. I took that suggestion to heart and studied typologies, including Astrology, the Enneagram, and Meyers-Briggs. Each taught me something about myself. And each framework eventually needed to be released, as useful but also limiting. Understanding one's personality is only a bridge to knowing Self.

Know Thyself has been said in different ways by different teachers. Ramana Maharshi, a 20th century Hindu sage and liberated being, taught the practice of asking "Who am I?" again and again. It was his road to enlightenment that he shared with his students.

The question leads much further than to a collection of facts. Learning about one's personality is only one part of the answer, and really not an answer at all. But it is a start. Behind the façade we have erected in response to this world, lay the more spiritual aspects of ourselves, where words are never enough.

13

The Meaning of Bird Wings

Manifestation

I knocked on the 'Shasta Daisy' door, one of many down the long hallway at Cluny, each named after a flower. It opened slightly and Joy peered out.

"Bon, come on in." She opened the door wider.

I was there to remind her that we were on the roster to cook this weekend. But what drew me in was her collection of shells, rocks, feathers, mossy branches, nests and bones spread across her room. Every bit of desk space and window ledge was covered and boxes lined the walls, filled to the top. A forest unfolded before me and I was speechless.

"Wow," I said. My eyes trailed along, drawn to the mysteries in each box. Joy explained that she had collected most while walking along the beach and hiking in the Cairngorm mountains.

Over on a table lay some feathers. I spotted a few iridescent streaks and looked closer.

"Are those bird wings?" They glittered in complex patterns of color, a subtle camouflage. "Beautiful."

I presumed finding undamaged bird wings was a rare occurrence. I had never come across a pair in all my years of hiking. And yet she had a collection of them. Looking once again at their beauty, I then turned back to remind her of our cooking day. I left carrying the image of those bird wings, and wondering how one finds a set.

It was not easy for me to enter Joy's door. She and I had history. Months before, as a long term guest, she joined our group, excited to help out in the veggie garden.

I liked her. She was a bit younger than I, a warm and friendly American, full of energy, who often broke out in peels of laughter. She had lived in South America, worked on ecological projects, and was a whirlwind of ideas and inspirations. Some tinges of envy arose in me as I heard of all her accomplishments while still in her twenties. I, who had dared to move to Scotland by myself in my thirties; had dared to join a spiritual community, overcoming fears and insecurities to get here. My later twenties had been focused on emotional survival. Her confidence rang loudly in my ears.

She brought to me a flurry of ideas, all aimed at creating a more ecological and sustainable garden plot. As the focalizer, I felt compelled to stay open and value her contributions. And of course her ideas were good ones. But my irritation rose, a pressure built up, with each new plan she presented. Her idea to bury the kitchen's food scraps in the garden rubbed me the most. I watched as she moved through the beds, shovel in hand, digging up soil. The tranquil and delicate relationship I had developed with my garden disappeared. That weekend, I went to Theresa, the garden's overall focalizer.

"I think I'm really wrong about this, but I just don't like her digging up the garden. It feels like her garden, not mine."

Theresa responded simply, "Tell her to stop then." She continued, "It is your garden, and you have every right to have it done your way."

My garden! The thought reverberated through me. In a community where all is shared, for this piece of time, the garden was mine. The garden at my home in Wisconsin was my father's creation, and I more of a thorn in his side, as I suffered the loss of every weed he pulled up. "You have to tell them ahead of time, and do it with love," I insisted, taking the concepts absorbed from the Findhorn garden book to an extreme. So here, in this very large community, I was given a chance to create a garden the way I wanted.

Armed with Theresa's authorization, I asked Joy to stop. It was not easy to explain why, but I did not waver. This was my garden space. My petty recalcitrance was there for all to see, but it was important for me to defend my right to have things my way.

So visiting her in her room was a bit of an olive branch. It was a few months after I stopped her, after she had joined another garden in another part of the community. Years later, she wrote a book of her time at Findhorn, and the episode of the food scraps was mentioned. I was embarrassed and could barely read how she depicted me. Resistant and uninformed, I imagined, which was true then. Little did she know what strength grew in me that day, a strength I needed for claiming my rights in the future.

And then there were those bird wings…

A few weeks after visiting her room, I got a chance to walk back to Cluny from the Park. It was a glorious, sunny day, rare in Scotland. Staying away from the well-traveled highway, I hiked down a farm lane by fields dotted with wildflowers, losing myself in the sultry warmth and clear blue skies.

It was my practice to pick up garbage by the roadway, and I had a few small wrappers in my hand. Up ahead I spied a plastic bag that was perfect for carrying the litter. As I grasped the handles, the heaviness surprised me, so I looked inside. It contained two large bird wings.

Was I seeing correctly?

They weren't exactly like Joy's. They were overall brownish-black, rather than rippled variations of color and pattern. Large and freshly severed, they had blood and muscle hanging off, not from a predator's teeth, but likely a human's hand.

I carried the bag to my bedroom, and arranged the wings on the sill of my window to dry up. A few mornings later I noticed they had disappeared, likely taken by some hungry animal. Or fallen into the lair of ants and worms and other creatures of the soil, to be transformed.

I never regretted their loss, their purpose already fulfilled. All I had learned about manifestation was second-hand from the experiences of the community's founder. But here was proof that manifesting was possible. I also learned a valuable lesson from the slight guilt bubbling up in my stomach. My reason for seeking bird wings was a frivolous one, a vanity. Losing them felt perfectly appropriate, considering how unimportant they were to my life.

Years later I found another pair of bird wings that held a more meaningful purpose. On a sunny afternoon, my boyfriend and I were walking down the narrow paths of Sacramento's river front, when suddenly he pulled me into a secluded area. "I think it's time we separate. I've thought it through carefully. I'm moving in another direction and want to be free to pursue my dreams."

The trajectory of our relationship had often fluttered, shifting with the changes in his life. Weathered by previous separations, I had gained a certain resilience to his leave-taking. I stayed silent, holding inside my intuitive sense that our deep connection would last over these ephemeral doubts of his. As we walked out from the pocket of grasses where we had sat, I spotted two bird wings, tiny wings, lying on the pathway. They were meant for us. I carefully picked them up.

"Here's one for you, and one for me. Like the bird who flew with these wings, I kinda suspect you won't fly too far away." And he did not.

Our relationship took many more turns before my willingness to continue petered out. Although we separated long ago, I've kept my tiny wing to this day, stored in a box with a snake skin, loose feathers, a nest and broken bird eggs, all meaningful in their own ways.

MANIFESTATION

Peter Caddy was a master of manifestation. He held to his vision and what he needed appeared. Wanting a patio, he prepared the framing, acting in faith despite having no money for the expensive bags of concrete required. Just as he completed the frame, a neighbor told him of some water-damaged cement sacks abandoned on the roadside. He carried them home and began pouring his patio, having scavenged enough to finish the project.

Creating a vision statement for manifesting is common in New Age circles. If you want a partner, envision the qualities you are looking for and send it out to the universe. I met my husband this way. I saw a bear of a man, laughing and kind and open to the spiritual beliefs I held. And my timing was right; I was ready to find a partner. I joined a computer dating service and met a few men this way. After almost a year of searching, I had enough and planned to withdraw. But I received a sign of interest from someone and gave it one more try. It was odd because my soon-to-be husband was ready to give up as well, and did not remember contacting me. When we met, so many of his traits clicked into place on my list, including the four I saw originally.

These examples of manifestation require a certain mindset, a belief in our capacity to draw to us what we need. Peter taught that maintaining a clear image was essential. Parking spaces appear for certain people who believe in their capacity and hold fast to the vision.

For those with less of an inclination for control, trusting the greater Spirit to bring us what we need without a clearly defined vision, is another way of manifestation. Faith is the binding glue, a faith that all our needs will be provided for.

Each success we experience expands our's confidence. And the outer world begins to look more supportive, more nurturing.

14

The Garden of Humans and Devas

Nature and Healing

The days were long and cool in the Scottish summers. Occasionally the clouds retreated and the sun warmed the sheltered vegetable garden enough to be considered hot. I would race up the dirt path to my room and change into one of the three pairs of shorts I had brought. Returning to the garden, I might have gotten fifteen minutes of sun on my legs before the skies changed. Clouds reemerged, blown across the island at a fast pace by the high winds. And underneath the illusion of warmth, created by the sun's rays, lay cold soil and cool air. I shivered my way back up the hill for pants. I may have worn my shorts three or four times in the five years I lived there.

Alison was from Edinburgh, and marveled at my legs. "You look like one of those blondes from California!" An image she had likely seen on the tellie or in a magazine. So few legs were ever shown in that cold clime.

Working in Cluny garden gave me a chance to try out some

of the ideas taught in *The Findhorn Garden*. There were ways of relating to nature with a greater sensitivity and respect. I was just a beginner, but intent is everything in a forgiving world.

The vegetables one grows in the Scottish summers were strangers to me. Having come from the Midwest, my dad and I always planted tomatoes and corn. Neither of those did very well at Findhorn. What grew abundantly were carrots, beets, leeks, potatoes and cabbage. The meals at Cluny were various combinations of these foods. So becoming acquainted with the new plants was one of my tasks.

When planting the seeds or when transplanting, I always welcomed the Deva, or over-lighting presence, of each kind of vegetable. Imagining a conscious being holding the pattern for carrots or cabbages took a bit of effort, and I acted in faith most of the time.

I tithed the last plant in each row to the animals and insects, and asked for their cooperation. "You are welcome to these plants but only these. Not the other ones, please. They are for us humans." Then they were given free rein to ravage the selected plants. It seemed to work, though if I wavered in my faith, the imagined protective shield would falter.

Peggy and I both had problems with the gophers, who loved to tear up the lower gardens. She focalized the perennial border, a walkway of flower beds along the hedge, and often found newly planted flowers unearthed. Annoyed by the damage the gophers had done to this strip of beauty, she growled and complained in our attunements. I had less of an issue with the gophers, but thought it better to act sooner than later. We decided to meditate together, thinking the added support may strengthen our case. Rodents are different than insects and they just might be less willing to cooperate, their habits harder to break. And we humans have our own fears and prejudices to deal with.

As I focused within, I saw a great gopher, an elder I think, his face appearing in the dark hole of his tunnel. A being to respect rather than soften with love. Yet with the respect came a love of sorts. I addressed him directly, "Could you and your family please leave this garden and move across the street into the un-mowed areas of the golf course?" I had garnered so much love for him by this time, it seemed anything was possible. And it worked. My vegetable beds were never bothered again. Possibly because she was in more of a battle with them, Peggy still struggled. It's hard to generate love when feeling so irritated.

I had a similar experience with the snails in my California garden. They were everywhere, scuttling under cover in the early morning light. Such an overpopulation was the sign of a garden out of balance. Picking them off my favorite plants, my love for them grew as I held them in my palm. I moved them to other, less valued greenery. Their populations soon reduced, and balance was restored in the garden.

I never experienced nature spirits at Findhorn. It was later in my life that the world of nature spirits became more apparent. We do need proof at times. Faith is not enough. And for me, opening the gate to a more subtle realm took true belief and an open heart.

One early winter morning, years after my time at Findhorn, I was planting out natives in my front yard. The sky was muted in grays, the air still and unusually silent. I prepared a potted sage. Sitting on my haunches, I noted the minute details of the greyed leaves. My heart was full of a mother's love as I placed the plant in position, envisioning it healthy and full of life. The whole garden area seemed to flourish before me. I was so grateful.

As I looked out over the remaining bare patches, and the broader neighborhood, I noticed, coming up the silent street, a whirlwind of dust. I watched in fascination as it skimmed the surface, collecting debris as it came closer. It moved onto my garden bed right in front of me. Reaching the middle, it picked up leaves, sending them past, ever circling, ever expanding, until I was in the midst of whirling leaves.

I knew, could never doubt again, that a nature spirit was sending me a message of greeting, hidden in the swirling air. It was the gesture of a lighthearted being, a subtle prankster. In awe, I watched it continue to encircle the plot, expanding to enclose me inside.

I wanted another witness, so slipped out of the ring and raced indoors. "Honey, come out and see the whirlwind in our yard." Usually groggy in the morning, John simply grunted in response. Having made the effort, I returned to the wind's display. Siting myself nearby, I kneeled, watching until the wind subsided and the leaves melted back into the landscape, into the stillness that was the day. I came away knowing each moment in nature carries the possibility of magic, if I am open to it.

Moving from job to job was common at the community. Theresa, Peggy and I were the only members of the garden group during the cold spring. Yet as the days warmed up, we expanded to include Robin, Rebecca and Alison. The six of us formed a tight knit group, supporting each other over the summer. Towards the end, Robin and Rebecca disappeared, moving into other jobs throughout the community. Peggy left as well, joining the Guest Department to lead Experience Weeks.

The last to depart was Theresa. She had enough of the community and was considering leaving for good. Her first step was to release focalizing Cluny Garden. In early fall, Theresa, Alison and I had gathered for our weekly attunement when she broke the news to us. An amazing season for me, the loss of the others was difficult. For Theresa to leave was heartbreaking. Yet as she let go, I felt an energy rise inside me, a sense of responsibility fill me.

"Alison, are you planning on staying?" I asked. She nodded. "Me too. I guess we're gonna be the ones to take care of the garden."

Theresa laughed and nodded towards me. "See, the angel of Cluny Garden has already found its new focalizer."

Oh that's what that energy was, I thought.

I looked to Alison. "Did you want to focalize?"

"Oh God, no. I am perfectly happy just being part of the team," she replied.

As the focalizer of a work department, I attended weekly meetings with the other department heads from housekeeping, maintenance, the kitchen, the dining room and reception. We discussed the running issues of the building. Pieter, the overall focalizer of Cluny, was the moderator. He led us in numerous decisions where we needed to come to a consensus. We used the same method that was used when the whole community decided to buy the caravan park. First discussing the issue, we expressed our opinions, then meditated to find the best answer for all concerned.

In our small group, our answers were almost always in agreement, even if we had felt differently before going into the silence. The best answer was not an answer we could think our way to. We had to surrender our own opinion and listen to a wiser source.

It was fall and the number of guests had diminished. The truth of the matter was, I didn't want any more guests. I was a bit on overload and needed a break. Yet we attracted two long term guests who helped us put our gardens to sleep for winter.

Kry came from Southern California, the daughter of a Japanese farmer. She laughed a lot in our gatherings, but had a depth that quivered near depression. She came down to work in the vegetable garden with me, wanting to weed silently. Weeding was the least important job in the garden, yet I recognized her need. Her long black hair draped down gracefully, as she carefully focused on each plant she pulled out. I watched with some frustration as she moved through the beds slowly, while the weeds around her grew fast.

I believe in holding a position of leadership one becomes a magnet, attracting those who are drawn to your energy. Tanya was from Germany. Despite my reticence for adding another guest to our roster, I agreed to meet. The meeting was a surprise. My magnet had brought me, kicking and screaming, face to face with my next challenge, loving Tanya.

NATURE AND HEALING

I spun out of control after seeing An Inconvenient Truth. Sobbing in the movie theater, I vowed to change my habits. I raced around my home the next day, turning off lights and replacing bulbs. My obsession only irritated my husband. "Hey, I can't see what I'm reading!"

My backyard became a respite. The peaceful scene soothed my panicked brain. The squirrels never stopped their search for food; the birds chirped their songs, and all was right in their world. They remained unaffected by the most devastating prediction I had ever heard. The only way I was going to make it through this crisis was to be out there with them as much as possible. I established a vegetable garden and planted natives to attract more birds, butterflies and bees. My gardening gave me a modicum of control over a dire situation.

A few years later, I was diagnosed with breast cancer. The morning after, I emerged a different person into a different world, a world where cancer dominated. I grabbed a hose and started watering my front garden, still a bit in shock.

Earlier that month, I had put two crepe myrtles in the ground at night, so the hot California sun would not stress them. The next day, I noticed they were misaligned. I shifted the lower one. Shortly after, its leaves yellowed and then fell, clearly shocked by my extra intervention. The plant's branches were empty sticks scheduled to be removed later.

That day, as I watered, I noticed a green speck on the dead bush. I thought it was a fallen leaf from the nearest tree, but went to check it out anyway. From the wood, a new leaf was emerging. Looking closer, I could see tiny green leaves shining in the light from all the branches. Life!

I spun around, seeing life bursting out from every corner of my yard. Love filled my chest. It was the love we felt for each other, my garden and I. I was held in its arms. It was then I knew all would be fine.

Nature is a healer. It is not that working in the soil or hiking in a forest purges us of our pain or straightens out our thinking. But taking a break from a frenetic world, and our frenetic mind, helps. The patterns of order, the innocence of birds, the warmth of the sun, they soothe us. Being around something innocent and pure can ease one's pressures, and bring hope in dire times.

15

There Is No Roadmap For This Kind of Thing

The Realities of a Relationship

I was in a friend's apartment, gathered with others. A knock sounded at the front door and I rose up to answer. A man stood in the hall. Although never having met him before, I knew him; loved him. We sat next to each other and I held his hand. It would have been impossible not to. An energetic bond flowed between us. It was like every cell of my body was linked to every cell in his. His thoughts were my thoughts, his words mine. He addressed the gathering, as if he was a teacher, then rose to leave. At the doorway he turned back to me. Without speaking, he sent the thought, "This is not a parting, for we will be together again." I did not need to respond. He knew me; he knew my heart.

For weeks after this dream, I felt held in love, a palpable love that was present every second of my day. I was not alone.

It took me years to assimilate this experience. Was he my soulmate? I thought so at the time. We were destined to meet later in life. Was he my other half, as described in Plato's idea of a split soul? Why else the strong magnetic feel to our connection? My sixteen-year-old, fanciful nature wrapped the concept of a soulmate in ideas of romance and marriage, like a maypole wrapped in colored ribbons.

Are they the one? I asked myself at every new encounter. And every time I knew they were not the *he* of my dream. My sister once said, "I thought I was your soulmate." And truthfully, she was. We seemed to have signed on to support each other through this life. My belief in soulmates slowly dissolved, one ribbon at a time.

Today, I see this dream differently. He was me, the me that is possible. Dream interpretations often consider every person in a dream to symbolize a part of one's self. He was wise, powerful and loving. How could I not want to re-find that part of me?

My search for a partner continued at Findhorn, because underlying my hopes of finding someone special was a very human yearning to be loved, to be understood, to be held. I kept on looking, not for a soulmate, but for someone to build a life with. It was a futile endeavor, because I wasn't ready. And some wiser part kept reminding me the task at hand was more about growing myself and less about finding a partner.

Alison told me a long-term guest had asked to join the Cluny garden group. Still reeling from the loss of so many members, all I could feel was tired. And over the busy summer, we had up to fifteen new guests join us each week: people to support as they adjusted to the community, people to find jobs for, and people to say goodbye to on Fridays. I looked forward to the winter, when the days were shorter and the garden quieter.

Alison arranged the meeting with Tanya. I just had to drag my feet to the busy dining room. After we filled our trays with lentil loaf and salads, she led me to the table where a dark-haired girl was sitting, who grinned broadly as we sat down.

Alison was directly across from her and did most of the talking. I listened in from the side, sometimes following their conversation but easily distracted by people at the other tables. Occasionally Alison drew me back in by asking for my opinion.

Tanya laughed heartily. She had a solidity to her, like she would be comfortable anywhere. She spoke English with a slight German accent. My worries were eased. She would be a good fit for our little group.

At the end of lunch, we arranged to meet at the Sanctuary on Thursday afternoon, where we would meditate to 'tune' her in. As we rose to go, I walked around the table and reached out for a hug. And for the first time, I truly looked at her.

The scene seemed to freeze as my shock registered. I recognized her. Not her face, but her essence. She was important; she would be important.

Of course, nothing was said. I perked up, suddenly very interested. An adventure was starting, and it was unclear where it would take me. From then on, I was acutely aware of her.

On Thursday, in meditation, we envisioned Tanya entering our circle. Afterwards, I grabbed her hands and leapt up and down. *Who am I? Just a few days ago I was asleep with indifference, not wanting anyone new.* She felt the excitement too and jumped as well. Our little group became a foursome that day.

It is a rarity, finding people in life we recognize. The

recognition is not through our memories but comes from deeper within. I was not sure what the nature of our relationship would be. The powerful draw I felt towards her only made me more cautious. I wanted to ease in slowly.

As we got to know her, Alison and I were continually surprised. A medical doctor, Tanya worked in a unit of a Hamburg hospital that specialized in Anthroposophical medicine based on the teachings of Rudolf Steiner. "Wow," we both exclaimed in unison.

Doctors appeared to me as distant authority figures, busy and burdened and driven by their role. Tanya held her profession as simply one of many aspects of herself, including her skill as a musician. It was as if her doctor role was a spinning top she balanced on her finger, something she played with. She was a warm, friendly, very human being, with great emotional depth. Her eyes sparkled mischievously, as if nothing was important enough to take so seriously one forgot the joys in life. She laughed a lot, but there was a quietness about her as well, and a self-possessed wisdom.

We mainly talked in the garden, and saw each other at lunch sometimes. At one point Tanya had the flu. I never reached out personally to the guests, so was surprised to find myself visiting her in her bedroom. She had other visitors as well and we all chatted. I recognized the depth of my feelings by that act. I was taking our relationship to another level.

One evening, I walked past while she looked at the bulletin board after dinner. Impulsively, I wrapped my arms around her from behind, and bended my knees into the back of her knees. She folded and I held her. It was an intimate, spontaneous act. We laughed and enjoyed the moment.

Shortly after, she put a note under my door. "I'd like us to go a little further." I didn't know what she meant. Of course she didn't know either. An unspoken passion was driving this relationship. The next day she came to the vegetable garden. I carefully avoided answering her message. We skimmed around the huge empty space between us, focusing on composting and weeding. One could feel the tension building from my holding back and her growing frustration. Finally, at the end of her rope of tolerance, she threw the watering can at me. I knew why without her saying a word.

Suddenly our moving forward was inevitable. I gathered her in my arms to calm her and whispered, "I would like to go further too." Although I had no way to know if we were heading in this direction, I did ask, "Have you been in a relationship with a woman before?"

"No" she said.

"I have. One time before." It was left at that.

We went on an adventure that weekend, biking out into the countryside on a warm afternoon. We climbed trees and talked about our lives. That night we became lovers.

Although I preferred men sexually, I didn't know how to express the intensity of my feelings in another way. We never planned for this. Love and the desire to be with each other drove our actions forward, and we followed.

As winter approached and the nights grew longer, I planned to return home after the long year of being a new member. Tanya came with me to visit my mother in Chicago. Then we flew to my sister's home in California. My sister knew, even before we descended off the plane, that Tanya would be someone important, not just to me, but to her. We spent the vacation in continuous adventure, riding horses on the beach and hiking in the redwood forests. Driving south to Mexico, we roamed the seashore of the Baja. After our trip, Tanya returned to Germany and I to the gardens of Cluny Hill. Both of us had our paths to walk.

If the purpose of loving Tanya was to wake up my heart, that would have been gift enough. However we had signed on for something more profound that occurred between us a few years later.

THE REALITIES OF A RELATIONSHIP

I was raised on Disney princess cartoons and stories of romance. Love at first sight was a common occurrence in my imagination, and I romanticized every possible relationship. Reading of soulmates only added fuel to my fervor.

In my later years, after letting go of my unrealistic notions of romance, I realized a permanent partnership must ultimately be practical. Loving is more important than being in love. Similar values, similar cultures help extend the time shared together. Opposites are stimulating and teach us a lot, but without some similarities, we have so little to build on. And I often reminded my clients of the structure being built, the ship of the relationship, meant to sail through life together and weather the stormy seas.

Relationships, begun early in one's life, forces us to face ourselves and our partners. In my marriage, occurring in the latter years of my life, entering that petrie dish of change was less important. My husband and I, instead, faced the world together. We made a good team, a description I would never have thought to use when I started dating thirty years before.

16

Leaning Into Others

Co-Dependency

I loved Cluny Garden, but staying in one work position at the community was not possible for me. Each year I shifted departments, changing and advancing to fit my needs at the moment. Working in the garden had a simplicity to it, where my nerves could settle as I put my hands in the soil. Adapting to the high stimulus of community life took me some time. My next job would position me right in the nerve center of the place.

It had been over a year since becoming a member. One day, in early spring, Anna slid into the chair opposite me at lunchtime.

"Bonnie," she said, starting into her question immediately.

I had known Anna in passing, but she appeared aloof and inscrutable so did not know her well. We truly 'met' during an Easter conference held in the Universal Hall. Many of the membership were there. One particularly powerful exercise began with the audience forming a large oval on the central floor. Pachelbel's Canon played as we slowly moved past one another. Instructed to stay silent, we looked at the person opposite us for a few minutes, then moved on. The experience slipped away any vestiges of defensiveness in me. I looked into each person's eyes with an openness that saw into their essence. I was shaken to my core. Anna and I met that way. Her lips quivered and her eyes filled with tears; mine did also. To see her so vulnerable was lovely.

"Yes, Anna," I said, "What's up?"

"Hey, I need to ask you something. Would you like to co-focalize an Experience Week with me?"

I was surprised to be asked. We travelled in different circles. She lived with Pieter, the focalizer of Cluny. And she was the head of the Guest Department, the group that led Experience Weeks, Departmental Guest Weeks and the Long-Term Guest Months. These programs were the bread and butter of the Foundation, providing a chance for guests to integrate into the community.

Doubt was my first response. Could I actually lead a group? Unsure, I back pedaled. "Oh, I don't know. I've never done one."

"It's very easy. The format is fully structured, and I'll guide you," she offered. "I think you'll do well."

I took a deep breath. It was tempting, doing something new, something challenging. And it was only a week long. "Yeah, I'll do it."

We met a few days before the Week began to plan which members we would ask to participate in the evening talks. The rest was pre-structured.

Accommodations gave us the participants' autobiographical letters to read. On Saturday, we linked their description with their person, and could draw on that information if needed over the week. The mismatch between their self-description and how they acted over the week amazed me. *How deluded are we about ourselves?*

From the first session, I loved supporting people seeking more from their lives. Every evening they shared their process, each unique. I watched their unfolding under the transformative light of the community.

Feeling myself a part of their group, I often ate meals with them. Anna held back, was more reserved. She knew how to survive the many groups she would have to lead over the summer months. I innocently leapt in. Something must have gone right, for shortly after our week, she asked me to join her department.

"What about the garden. Who will care for it?" I asked. Spring had arrived and the pressure was on to get the vegetables planted out.

"People change departments all the time," she responded. "We'll find people to take on the garden. But you are someone who can do Experience Weeks, and we need you."

The population of guests increased dramatically during the summer time. Sometimes the community scheduled three Experience Weeks simultaneously. They needed me, clearly.

Alison, as well, supported my leaving the garden. "No, don't worry about me. Take your next step. The garden will survive."

Peter Caddy had often said that at first they grew vegetables, but later they were more about growing people. It amused me to think I was following the same path. In truth, I felt destined for something different than: working in a garden, or keeping a house, or assisting nurses to get their blood draws delivered to the lab. Something creative was wanting to emerge, and something different as well. I carried an energy of transformation, yet never knew quite how to bring that into my life. Holding the space for guests to gain insights and grow was the perfect job for me.

Starting in April, I focalized an Experience Week twice a month with a variety of co-focalizers. These were members of the community who volunteered to help.

I adored the people in my groups. Like a mother hen, I watched them open and grow. I worked to draw out the shy guests, and reached out to as many others as I could. Their sharings, although sacrosanct, gave me clues as to how they were handling the experience. On the last day, their summary of what they gained filled my heart.

During each Week, we took the group to hike along the Findhorn River. Grabbing the chance to be alone, I hurried along the path to get some privacy. On my first visit, I came upon a huge beech, a grandmother tree, jutting out into the river. Positioning my back against its smooth bark, I relaxed and let the sound of the rushing waters flow over me. It was then I noticed a feeling of energy rising up my back. It seemed to be coming from the tree itself, as if I could feel its rising sap. The energy felt good, so I visited the tree often over that summer.

Another time I found a huge conifer and thought to try its energy. The lower branches projected out, many of them dead, so I was not able to get close enough to place my back against the trunk. I sat on the ground instead. A tiredness crept over me and I nodded off, awakening drained and dull twenty minutes later. Perhaps trees have different effects on us. This one seemed to sap my energy.

My work cycle that summer shifted between times of expansion, when I led Experience Weeks groups, and times of contraction, empty weeks when I pulled back into myself. Like a sharp blade, the end of each group cut into my cords of attachment. Most of the guests I would never see again. The shifting sands of my job pushed me very quickly to toughen up around loss.

One interesting practice Anna shared was cleansing the workshop room after the group ended. We entered a meditative space then envisioned a light entering and filling the room. Any dark or out of place energies were removed, sent to the absorbing earth below us. This kind of imaginative magic also worked in setting up the protective fencing done at Cullerne.

I changed bedrooms when I changed jobs, moving into a room in the basement of Cluny, where other longer term members stayed. We were far away from the hubbub of people, and I needed that quiet time to recoup the energy that drained away during the times of noise and activity. On my off weeks, my days were spent taking long walks in the forest and along the country roads.

By August, I was comfortable with the rhythm of my work. Of course, being in a state of ease and comfort does not last long at Findhorn or in anyone's life if invested in growth. At the start of my ninth Experience Week, Sandy, my co-focalizer, and I described to the group what was scheduled for the week, as we had always done. A guest spoke up. "That sounds really boring. Can't we do something more fun?"

I was shocked. My shiny little world was getting jostled. No one, in my experience, had ever judged our program so negatively. Time and again, people trusted the process and at the end shared how much they enjoyed the Week.

I didn't know how to answer him.

Sandy replied, "Give it a chance. You may find it better than you are assuming it is."

Determined to win him over, I poured myself into the group. By the end of the week, I was exhausted. At the last meeting, he shared how wonderful the week had been for him. The magic of the community had worked. But my nerves were spent. I had leaned too far in, which only added to the leaning I did over the spring and summer.

It was Sunday, the day after I said my goodbyes to the group. I woke up overwhelmed, scheduled to lead the evening meditation, to do kitchen clean-up, and to start a Department Guest (DG) week, the first one I had ever done. Would I fail as the focalizer? And what if the critic from the Experience Week showed up in my DG group? What if he criticized my program? It was all too much.

I couldn't wrap my mind around doing the day. "I can't... I can't..." ran through my brain. Walking out the back of the building, I wasn't sure what to do. Tears streamed down my cheeks. Fred, part of the maintenance group, walked by. I tried to verbalize my panic, but could not get the words formulated. Bending over, I took in quick breaths of air. He fetched Roger, who immediately recognized my wreckage. I couldn't explain what was happening, did not know what I needed.

"Okay, we are sending you away from here. What are you supposed to do today?" Roger asked.

I managed to say between gasps, "Departmental Guest week...... sanctuary ....kitchen clean-up."

"Who can I call to get you?" he continued.

"Morley." *She has a car,* I thought. *And I feel safe with her.*

"Fred, will you stay with her? I'll call Morley and see if I can get people to fill in her shifts." Roger took off.

I leaned against a pillar to wait, unable to formulate the simplest phrases with Fred.

Soon Morley arrived and I was put in her car. We drove in silence the ten miles to Elgin, a town south of Forres. She parked by a broad expanse of beach on the North Sea. Just what I needed. I walked slowly towards the surf and listened to the gulls cawing, the wind blowing on my face, drying up my tears.

"Where do you want to go now?" Morley asked. "Can I take you to Cullerne?" This was where she stayed. I nodded.

I settled on a couch in the Cullerne House family room. Most of the time I was mute, my brain unable to form words. Other members said hi as they passed me by. I sat in their group around the dinner table, but could not make sense out of what they were saying. My brain had given up. My brain that had tried so hard to please others, just couldn't anymore.

I slowly recovered over the week. A 'nervous breakdown' I would call it. I had never experienced one before and never since. My brain needed rebooting, and the first thing I wanted to change was my overactive need to please others. I was done with that. It was the beginning of a long transformative year.

After that week, I returned to Cluny, but stayed away from leading groups. I took on simpler jobs, and planned a visit toTanya. I hoped my trip to Germany would give me a break from the intensity of this last summer.

CO-DEPENDENCY

Co-dependents were common in my practice. These people focused on pleasing others, while ignoring their own needs. A variety of problems emerged for my clients who struggled with this relational disorder. Anxiety, depression, guilt, and anger accompanied their robotic willingness to be used by others.

The term was first coined in reference to enablers, usually family members of alcoholics and drug users. The substance abusers let their responsibilities go, and the enabler picked up the pieces, trying to hold the other's life together. The term co-dependency has since been broadened to include a variety of situations. What they all have in common is an imbalanced relationship.

I illustrated this imbalance for my clients, by holding my two hands upright in front of me, palms facing each other about two inches apart. They represented two people interacting normally. When both stayed grounded within themselves, they remained upright and the center of the relationship lay between them. Then I showed a co-dependent relationship. The center of the relationship was on the helped. The helper's hand leaned so far towards the other, they could not keep their own balance. If the helped person left, the co-dependent fell.

So many women learned helper behaviors from their mother. My mother trained me similarly. I never struggled with co-dependency before leading groups. But focalizing Experience Weeks brought those long buried behaviors of the helper out in me. I imitated my mother, shadowing her tendency to over-extend herself with others.

Keeping centered within oneself is always the best. I had to learn this the hard way, and endeavored to teach my clients how important inner balance was for them.

Change is not easy for those married to the concept of being there for others. The guilt and anxiety the co-dependent feels when they fail to help is often unendurable. For some, it is their whole purpose for living. They rationalize that attending to their own needs is selfish. Many people on spiritual paths get caught in these viewpoints, having the belief that love means being there for others to the detriment of oneself.

Clients usually sought me out when their tendency became obsessive, their emotional pain intractable. I suggested my clients begin to change by answering a request for help with "Let me think about it" first. That way they have the time to give a well-thought out answer, rather than an automatic "Yes." I helped them see that if we do not care for ourself first, we cannot effectively care for another. A perfect reminder is given every time we fly; parents are told to put on their own oxygen masks before attempting to put on their children's.

17

A Solar Fire

Ideas of God

I looked God straight in the eye, and with all the vehemence I could muster, yelled "Fuck you!" The cows grazing in the field next to me bore witness to my daring. I expected a lightning bolt or two. But the cows kept on eating, and the skies stayed a steady grey. A fire started in me that day; the flames in my heart reduced my love for God to ash. The emerging rage dwelt so deep within, it took months to extinguish.

I had just returned from visiting Tanya in Germany, a much needed respite. Exhausted after a summer of leading Experience Weeks, my time as a Guest Department focalizer ended in a breakdown that ripped my kind and caring façade away. I was not so amenable on my return: tired of serving, tired of helping others out, and angry to be so drained. Cluny felt like a cage of expectations, restricting my movement.

My power was waking up. I wanted to declare freedom from

the world server role previously donned. It wasn't that the qualities of kindness and caring weren't a part of me, and being a world server wasn't an ideal I still strove for. The truth of these qualities within I would discover later. But for this time, I needed freedom from their demands.

Soon after returning, Karin cornered me in the hall. A husky German in her forties, she radiated a matriarchal authority. Recently, she had taken over the focalization of Cluny from Pieter.

"What job would you like?" she asked, a perfectly appropriate question on my return. Yet I looked at her blankly, feeling lost and unsure of my next step. She continued, "We need someone to take on the focus for Housecare."

"Housecare? Oh no, I don't want to do that." I planted my feet. Too many years I had spent working as a cleaner.

"We need you to do this. We have no one else."

In the members' meeting that night I reluctantly agreed, not an ounce of willingness in me. Unlike my previous work departments, chosen carefully in meditation, this one felt forced. Yet I had no better option. And they needed me.

That weekend, I stomped along some roads and paths that lay near Cluny, ranting to myself as I passed fields with cows grazing. My view was blotted by my anger. I once hoped to find a life partner here, but loneliness clawed at my heart. Brimming with potential, here I was in Housecare, trapped doing a job performed since childhood. I wanted what I wanted, and was tired of surrendering to God and accepting what came. The God who guided my path and gave me what I needed, had failed me.

A rage rose in my chest and I looked straight into God's

eyes, "I have gotten nothing from You. You can get fucked! I am doing it on my own from now on." A deep determination arose, steeling my insides. "No more ... Fuck You!" I would not soften.

That day a burning started in my heart. Grey clouds moved to block the sun as my insides flamed crimson red. And yet the cows continued grazing, unaffected by my shattering vow.

Focalizing Housecare was not a difficult job, just rote. I tried to find some fulfillment by improving the appearance of the vacant guest rooms. Moving furniture, switching out curtains and pictures, I could not bring harmony to rooms that were built for two but had beds for four. Compulsively working to reorganize the spaces each evening, I only felt frustration and increased depression.

All the while, the fire was growing in my heart. I had stopped meditating, unwilling to converse with my made-up God. I couldn't calm down enough to find peace within, anyway. Yet the burning in my heart was puzzling. What did it mean?

Shortly after starting in Housecare, the cyst at the base of my spine swelled up. This had happened a few times over my life, only to recede by carefully avoiding pressure on it. I tried the same method, but the pain and heat increased, until my backside swelled and my body bended forward. Again, Roger came to my rescue. He insisted we go to the hospital, where I was rushed into surgery. They lanced my cyst, allowing a dark pus to drain.

I recovered in a large room, shared with three Scottish women. I was a bit of a novelty, an American and from 'that community'. My vegetarian meals were delicious, a blend of grilled fresh vegetables, unlike the limp, meat-based hospital meals provided for the others. The cook had been a chef in

London and was happy to branch out beyond the dictates of hospital food.

I asked Katie to bring my copy of Lonesome Dove and read large swaths of the book, enjoying the absence of pressure. The fire, which started the day of my divorce from God, continued to burn in my heart, lying in secret underneath my very normal conversations and interactions.

Occasionally I ignored the hospital rules by sneaking outside to soak in the sunlight. The sun! It was an intimate friend. In the light, the flames grew to fill my body. As I stood outside in my hospital gown, looking up at the sun's brilliance, a hot love poured from my heart. *Amazing how close rage and love are.*

A week later I returned to Cluny to recover further, staying in my bedroom in the basement most of the time. Healing takes energy and I couldn't do much else. Backaches, leg pains and an enduring cough plagued me. Whenever I crawled to the dining room, multiple people asked about me. I repeatedly answered, "not good." There was not much more we could talk about, as I lived in my own world and didn't know what was happening in the community. But this only added to the frustration that lay inside me. "Please stop asking!" I said on more than one occasion. Tired of playing nice with others, I did not care who knew it. My nerves were on edge whenever I left the haven of my room. It was time to leave Cluny.

A room in Drumduan, the grey stone building a short walk through the forest, became available. It had housed the Healing Workshop I attended when still a guest. Upstairs were members' quarters. The quiet of the house soothed my mood, the air clear of others' energies. I stayed in silence during most of my time there.

When my energy increased, I returned to Housecare, but my days lacked inspiration. Without God to speak to, without the heights of Spirit to aim for, the sky always seemed an overcast grey, even when sunny. My anger subsided but rose quickly when any semblance of entrapment, such as being pressured to volunteer, came close.

Katharina visited one evening, to help me sort through and understand my feelings better. We spoke of leaving the community as an option. But was it the right time?

On a sunny afternoon, I lay on the green lawn below Cluny and watched the clouds roll by. Thoughts of life in California drifted past and my solar plexus area joined those clouds, as though I were being pulled out of the community. Feeling lost these days began to make sense. It was time to go. I was ready. I would focus on building a career.

I set the date for late March. My friends took me to the local pub, giving me a wonderful send-off. It was the kind of send-off that makes one think about staying.

A few days before departure, I passed JT in the Cluny foyer. He had been at Findhorn awhile, and worked in Management. "I hear you're leaving," he said. I was surprised he even knew who I was. "I hope it all works out, but I think you'll be back. It doesn't feel like you are quite finished here." A perceptive man, I valued his comment, but placed his words in a limbo place. If he was right, I would be back. Moving forward was all I could do.

IDEAS OF GOD

I first learned of God in grade school. I loved the idea of a great Being watching over us all. God became the kind, accepting father I could look up to; a Man of light, whose rays shone through the clouds. But mostly, He became the arbiter of my life, the Being I prayed to for help, whom I thanked when something good happened.

As I grew older, my ideas of God changed. Exposure to other religions, and the many stories of enlightened people I had read, painted a different picture. I thought the concept of a discrete Being separate from me was unlikely. That we are all part of the divinity of life was more in step with my expanding views. But it took me time to grasp. I could envision an abstract beingness that encompassed the universe. But emotionally I still needed a lap to crawl into, a divine brother to hold my hand, and angelic beings to soothe my fears. Were these beings real? It didn't matter, for I used these imagined entities as tools to help me through my hard times.

One tool was not particularly useful, and became a hindrance for me: the role of God as arbiter. Developed in childhood, this became my superego, dictating what I should and shouldn't do. If I pleased God, I felt better. If I failed, I felt guilty. 'God the arbiter' lay unconscious but potent in my thinking and emerged into my awareness as I struggled for my own power. This was the 'God' I battled within myself.

As a therapist, I often suggested my clients find something greater to believe in and aspire towards. Developing such beliefs carry hidden benefits. Having faith in an abstraction like a religion, nature, or humanity gives us a chance for hope. It organizes and stabilizes our experiences, and creates a sense of purpose. And most importantly, it keeps our egos in check. Believing in something greater is humbling. Without belief, we float without direction. And more than that, we must bear our burdens by ourselves. Even if imagined, giving one's burdens up to something greater can be a relief.

18

My Will Versus God's Will

The Journey of Transformation

I want to go back! Every night I cried in my dreams. The homesickness was almost unendurable. And every morning, I grit my teeth and curled up my fingers, strong against the message my soul was giving me. My anger had diminished, as if cooled by the clean, ocean winds, but my will remained. I was determined to direct my life from my own decisions, not from some unconscious compelling. Though the guidance from my dreams was so apparent, I ignored it.

The tight grip on my spiritual side made for a dulled, grey feel in all my interactions. Yet my heart continued to burn with a dark red fire, and the self that held such strength and passion was just as easy to access. My will drove me on. I was a powerful being that looked to no one else.

I was living with my sister near the Pacific coast. My days were spent taking long walks by the ocean and exploring the farm lands nearby.

After three months of rest, I flew to London, and stayed at a friend's place near Hampstead Heath. She was spending her summer at Findhorn, and the place was mine to use. Every day I walked through the Heath, exploring large areas of wild lands, cultivated parks and pools. Nature was my constant and only companion, holding me steady as I attended the Psychosynthesis Essentials.

A therapeutic workshop, it utilized guided imagery as one of its tools in healing and personal growth. A Psychosynthesis workshop was given in the community and the leader's skillful way of guiding a person to look at their core issues impressed me. Intending to apply for the leadership training program, I hoped to wield transformative insights for others with as much compassion and instinct as I saw the trainers do.

The night before the workshop started, I had a dream. *I overheard my father say to my mother, "I don't want to lose Bonnie. Tell Bonnie not to give up on me." In my dream, I knew I must lose my father, that I wouldn't survive if I didn't.*

A few days into the weeklong program, I was part of a group session led by Fiona, one of the therapists. There were about fifteen of us, sitting in a circle, surrounded by pillows, in a large cave-like room with windows too high to look out of.

Fiona had a soft intelligence, unlike the brilliant, sharply perceptive mind of Robert, the workshop leader. She worked with us as individuals, gently and with compassion, while the rest watched. By the time her large eyes turned to ask how I was doing, I fully trusted her.

Feeling sluggish, I noted my ambivalence. "Well, my mind is curious and excited to be here, but my body doesn't want this."

"Ask your body what it wants," she suggested.

I imagined speaking to my body, and received this: "I don't like being invaded by others. I want to hide. I feel so powerless."

"It sounds like there is some anger. Do you feel angry?" she asked.

"Ah, no I don't... I don't feel that. I seldom get angry," I answered, forgetting to mention the months of rage I had gone through recently. "If I was angry at anyone, it would be my father."

"Okay, let's look into your relationship with your father," she said. "Imagine him sitting here." She had pulled up a chair and placed it opposite my seat.

Seeing my dad across from me touched deep into my heart. My eyes teared up. I loved this man. But other feelings were there as well.

"What is he saying to you?" Fiona asked.

I spoke aloud the words that came to me. "I loved you so much as a little girl, Bonnie. You were adorable. But I didn't like seeing you grow up, becoming opinionated and sexually freer. I'm not comfortable with you as an adult."

Through my tears, I spoke my response, "I love you too and want to please you. But I can see how you've held me back. I feel squelched and low around you."

I noticed a band of pressure across my chest building up, followed by a wave of energy rising up from my feet. Telling Fiona about this, she suggested I breathe into the sensations and allow them space. At first I got a bit dizzy. But the energy grew stronger, unrelenting. It stood me up and raised my arms. From deep within me a NO rose. The NO came from my body, pulsating with energy. I yelled out, "NO!" "NO!" I stomped my foot. "NO MORE!"

Fiona placed a pile of pillows in the center of the circle. "Let your energy out on these." Not caring who was watching, I began hitting out at the pile.

"Verbalize what you feel," Fiona prompted.

"I'm not gonna do it anymore!" I cried out as I slugged my imaginary enemy. "I'm not gonna do it!" Soon I stopped hitting the pillows and began sobbing. She immediately stepped in. "Don't pull back your anger. Don't do that to yourself. Get it out."

I lifted up my head, my body rippling with rage and looked at my father, who stood in front of me in my imagination. "You Asshole!" I reached up and grabbed him by the necktie, holding it in my hand, and pleaded with him, "Look at me. Talk to me. I'm so sick of you walking away. I am a woman and I want you to accept me."

Fiona asked why I was clenching my hand.

"I'm holding his necktie. I'm forcing him to look at me."

"Ask your father what he would like to say to you."

I waited for a response, but all I saw was him edging towards the door.

"Can you accept your father wanting to follow his way? Can you let him go, so he can go on his path?" Fiona asked.

At first I was afraid. "If I let him go, I might let go of myself as well. But I'll try."

I opened my fingers, one by one, releasing him slowly while endeavoring to keep my power in me. I watched him drift away while my power stayed.

Fiona asked me to receive a symbol for this experience. An

American Beauty Rose, a symbol of love, appeared in my mind, complete with protective thorns.

I emerged from my inner reverie and saw the whole class watching me, utterly present. They had followed my process while I was oblivious of them. I grinned, feeling light as a breeze and happy.

"Well, I think we've come full circle," Fiona chimed in. We all laughed.

After the Essentials workshop ended, I applied for the three year training course. While waiting for the decision, I roamed the Heath and explored other parts of London. A few days later a letter came; I was placed on a waiting list. It was a gut punch to my dreams. I was not prepared to hang around London, waiting to be accepted. The obstacle of the wait felt like an uncrossable barrier. Floundering about, I was lost. If not this, what should I be doing?

In the apartment was a pamphlet on Free Will by Roberto Assagioli, the founder of Psychosynthesis. He differentiated between self-will and God's will. Self-will comes from our mind and is a pushing sort of will, while God's will comes from the belly, with no pushing, just a knowing, a rightness. It was clear my self-will had been calling the shots over the last months.

My resolve to make my own way, to build my career, melted during those first hours. My walls dissolved and the waters of Spirit flooded into my body again.

It seemed walking this life alone, isolated from Spirit, hadn't work. I was eternally unhappy. My little self might have won a few battles but there was never, ever a chance that it would win the war, a war that never really existed except in my own mind. I had come to the community powerless, with a nature that leaned so far into pleasing others that I burned myself out. Winning back my power required rejecting all the values I had been taught, the façade of being a good person, a polite person. But now power was mine, my gut was strong. Strong enough that I could accept whatever life brought me, knowing it would be right for my growth. I could be vulnerable now.

I felt the pull to return to Findhorn. It wasn't my time to pursue a career. I had more to learn. And, oddly enough, the image of Gerd popped up; his name repeated in my thoughts. A newer member of the community, he was someone I only knew in passing. Yet, he would be in my future, clearly.

THE JOURNEY OF TRANSFORMATION

Could I have found my way without this battle against Spirit? Without rejecting the voice within for a period of time? Would I have been happy just accepting what came? Not likely. It felt inevitable, my stepping all in, allowing my rage, letting my rational self be shoved aside. After this process of winning back my power, a different person emerged.

Most people do not take such a journey. But I have admired many of my clients who pursued healing and won a stronger sense of self. Some are forced to change because of an addiction. Others had this journey thrust upon them in the guise of an assault or other trauma. They climbed their mountain of challenges with difficulty. They hung onto the thread-bare ropes of a more positive view of themselves or of life, ropes that often broke and had to be recreated. Each re-creation added to their strength, each success I saw as a triumph. For completing the path is not guaranteed, and most times just being on the journey reaps reward.

19

A Findhorn Homecoming

The Search For Love

The train was fast. The treeless moors and Scottish Highlands whizzed by, white and brown dots of sheep barely noticeable. The closer to Inverness, the stronger the pull in my chest. How different from when I left: so hard, angry, and fierce in my independence. I was returning soft, surrendered, not master but student again.

Letting go of my desire to be something important, I was humbled. Letting go of my resentments, I was willing. Letting go of my demands on God, I was open.

The thought of Gerd continued to draw me, his presence ever in the background of my mind. I barely knew him, yet my soul was telling me he would be important. What that looked like, or why, was in question.

It was late in the day when the bus dropped me at Cluny. Accommodations had found me a room at Drumduan. It was perfect, quiet and isolated. The intensity of Cluny all day and all night did not feel quite right. Walking the forested path to the grey stone mansion settled me after the long journey from London, and would settle me after long days of work.

There was a magic attending my steps. By saying yes to God, yes to continuing my inner journey, I knew my needs would be met. Gratitude and magic went hand in hand. How could someone feel so supported and not be grateful?

I left my bag in the bedroom and returned to Cluny for dinner. My steps to the dining room were punctuated with warm greetings.

After dinner, I joined the kitchen cleanup crew to say my hellos. We hugged and I teared up, happy to be back. As we talked, Gerd entered. He smiled, seemed glad to see me, yet neither of us took it any further. Whatever lay between us would unfold as it was meant to.

I slipped right back into community life, by focalizing an Experience Week starting a few days after my arrival. It was a breeze. I did not lean forward, but sat back and held my own, taking as much personal space as needed. My previous mistake in leading groups was apparent. An introvert, I behaved as my extroverted mother would have, and burned myself out.

During the Week's nature sharing, our speaker passed around a basket of objects from the forest and asked us to choose one. I was drawn to a large acorn. We were to first examine, then imagine ourselves as that object. Given pencil and paper, my impressions were: *I am brimming with excitement, full of potential waiting for the right soil, the right conditions. I feel the importance of my roots – they have to get going, to get strong so all of me can be nourished, can develop leaves and eventually nuts.* Imagining myself as an acorn made the action of planting a seed a living experience. Yet it was also a metaphor for why I returned to the community. Flowering and fruiting takes time. My roots needed longer to grow.

Gerd was asked to share his spiritual journey for the Inner Life segment. He began a little clumsily, but a shyness soon gave way to his wisdom. Unknown to me before, Gerd's inner life was rich, and I was moved by his words. Next, we were led in a meditation, and he concluded by suggesting we send out our love. Like a torpedo, a strong burst of energy shot out of my body towards him, and then diffused into the circle.

After completing the Week, I was adrift, without a job. While walking to the dining room Sunday morning, Ian pulled me aside.

Ian was very British, taking the time to enunciate perfectly every word of his Queen's English. He dressed neatly, often wearing a cravat tucked into the neckline of his sweater. Ian led an informal group in zen meditation. I did not last long, for staring at a blank wall in silence made me nauseous.

While he was the epitome of social propriety, he seemed to enjoy my blunderings, such as asking too personal a question or making a blunt comment. Little Loren's ribald dances on the kitchen table delighted him. "Americans!" he was probably thinking, while he laughed.

This morning he looked at me as if he had a brilliant idea. "Would you be interested in working in Communications? I'm leaving and think you would be a great fit."

The job entailed maintaining connections with people who previously visited the community from all over the world. It felt perfect. Rather than dealing with large groups of guests, my work would consist of letter writing and organizing files. Also, I would be there to assist visitors who wished to find connections in their country. Ann, who had been in Communications for many years, focalized the department.

"Yes," I said to him later that evening. The next day Ann met with me. She suggested I oversee the network of Resource People in North and South America. (Resource People, or RPs, are previous members or visitors who have offered to provide information about Findhorn to those living in their area.)

Ian must have been purging his responsibilities, for he approached me again a week later. "Would you like to take on the focus for Cluny library?" I loved libraries so leapt at the chance.

The library was behind glass doors off the second floor mezzanine. A small room, it was lined with shelves of books. The collection was always being updated as people often donated their books when preparing to leave. What a pleasure, to explore and keep organized the tiny collection.

I discovered a series of lectures there, offered to the community by the International Pathwork Foundation. A channelled collection, each volume was built on the previous one, taking a person deeper into themselves. Over the next few months, my evenings were spent reading, slowly digesting and contemplating each paper. At the same time, I was experiencing the unfolding of my friendship with Gerd.

I first met Gerd through Katie, an American, who had become one of my best friends. We met in an EST Communications Workshop, partnering in an exercise where we shared our deeper wounds. Katie had suffered sexual abuse and I was in tears by the end of her story. Her body was large, a protection of sorts, yet it did not dull her spirit. Her brown eyes sparkled with life. And she was one of the wisest people I knew, psychically gifted and perceptive.

Katie and I shared a love of crude humor. One evening we watched a one-star movie called *Johnny Dangerously*, starring Michael Keaton, with a group of friends. It was a stupid comedy and no one liked it except she and I. We lost our breath, laughing at the silliness.

Gerd was in her Orientation group, along with Richard. The three of them had formed a small study group, discussing books and meditating together. Richard, a British native, was sensitive and kind. His shy smile hid a depth few were privy to. He maintained a quiet aloofness, and Katie loved to verbally tickle him to get a laugh. In the future, Richard would swear off the New Age path and join a conservative Christian group.

Gerd was from Germany and had the feel of a priestly scholar. His longish dark curls were pushed back off his forehead and on his aquiline nose balanced metal-rimmed glasses. Baggy clothes hung on his thin frame and a book was often in his hand. An Aries, like me, his face flushed red when he was excited or frustrated. He laughed easily, with a nerd-like yuk-yuk.

One evening, I joined a group of friends, including Gerd, talking in the kitchen. As we chatted, an energy flowed between us, as if an alignment was forming. From then on, he was in the sanctuary when I meditated and he sat with me at dinners. His attentiveness made me cautious. My effort to stay focused on my own path was working. Losing myself in another person wasn't what I wanted.

On the weekend, Gerd and I decided to hike at Sluie's Walk along the Findhorn River. We met in the sanctuary before the trip. I was nervous; my insides were shivering, forcing me to be open and vulnerable. Although a head's up on where this was going would have been nice, my wiser self said *"Just surrender any need to know the future and be with what is."* My usual habit was to observe, understand and label. I was being told my relationship with Gerd would not be so easy to categorize.

We meditated, then got into his little Citroën to drive out to the Findhorn River. Walking along its banks, I shared my experience of the two trees, the one that energized me when my back was placed on its trunk, and the one that sapped my energy when laying near it. "I don't know if that can be true," he said. Perhaps not, but to this day placing my back on the trunk of old trees feels wonderful.

We climbed on boulders to get closer to the river, the sound of crashing water drawing us in.

"Oh, here is a perfect rock. Let's sit," I said.

We scrambled onto a large flat boulder that overlooked the river's rapids. I lazily spread out while Gerd sat upright. The warmth from the sun was soothing and sensual. Desire swept thru me, lying next to Gerd. Yet, next to his delicate sensibilities, I felt large and clumsy. We will not be in a physical relationship; this was clear to me. My desires were sent outward to savor the nectars of nature, and of life.

I remembered the message I received in London, in an exercise speaking to a wiser part of myself. My vision was of a kindly older man and I asked about my future. He said, *"You are alone and need to be alone in order to learn of your abilities. Only after you have proven you can manage by yourself, will it be appropriate to join with another."* It was this message I would cling to, while the gale force winds of my physical and emotional needs tossed me about.

THE SEARCH FOR LOVE

The search for love loomed large in my thoughts when I was younger. Yet forming my life around a hope for love from a fallible human was a fool's errand. Disappointment came too often. And certainly I wasn't ready to offer the unconditional love I hoped to find in another.

I read a phrase during my time at Findhorn that helped me reorient my thinking. "Give til the Lord stops giving to you." The love I looked for could only come from Spirit. And the path for receiving lay in the giving. The more I gave, the more I had to give. Love flowed through me, from my soul into this living world. Every time I was tempted to look toward another for fulfillment, I reminded myself where the true source lay.

In my practice, many clients felt empty inside, having gotten through childhood without the unconditional love they needed to grow their heart area. Heartbreak was common, after their futile efforts to seek reassurances from another that they were lovable. Eventually they sought out counseling to begin the work of rebuilding themselves. Their self-esteem had been severely wounded by that point.

The hard truth was they couldn't go back to make the past different. They were adults, not children anymore. The only way to fill their emptiness was to generate it from within. I helped them imagine their inner child, who did not get enough, and allow their love and compassion for this child to grow. For the path to self-esteem can be fueled by others, but ultimately it begins with the self.

20

My Dark Night of the Soul

Feeling One's Feelings

I dreamed I met a group of naked friends, cavorting in a stream. Joints were shared; music was talked about. Yet the stream beckoned me further. A few friends came with. The water was filled with garbage and feces. I went first, clearing a path for the others. Eventually the stream of waste turned into a tunnel. Pieces of the structure slid away as we scrambled upward. Finally we entered a huge stone room, part of a castle-like building high in the mountains. As I looked out over the coniferous forest, the building began shaking and swaying, the walls crashing around us. Like a sinking ocean liner, the floor lifted. I managed to grab onto a more solid part of the structure, and watched my friends tumble back down the hill. I realized, as I looked out over the snowy landscape, that I was alone, and would have to survive in this spot all winter.

Winters in northern Scotland were dark and long. At the solstice, the sun set about four in the afternoon and rose around eight in the morning, surrounded by hours of dusk.

Occasionally the northern lights danced along the skyline in blues and greens. Storms blew through quickly, the howling winds driving rain onto the granite buildings and small caravans that housed warmth and the gathering of people.

My life felt balanced. After a day of work at the Communications Office and the many social interactions one has over breakfast, lunch and dinner, I walked down the dark forest path, feeling my way to Drumduan. Entering the blackened forest without a light, each foot was placed carefully to ensure I stayed on the path. Every moment required my awareness. I had no fear, placing my trust in the darkness.

Upon entering Drumduan, I grabbed a cup of herbal tea in the kitchen, then took the stairs to my room, settling on my bed with a Pathwork paper.

The papers, channeled by Eva Pierrakos, were the result of her inner connection with a guide. As described on the lectures page of the Pathwork website, they are "a roadmap to self-responsibility, self-knowledge and true self-acceptance." They required that one faces ones "self-doubt, self-hatred and fear of inadequacy."

Immersing myself in the material, each concept presented was considered carefully. *"Is this something I do?"* In the quiet of my evenings, I faced myself directly, faced the uglier parts of me.

Usually seen as the good girl, the white sheep of our family, I was forced to admit my capacity for hatred and envy. The proof was in my memories of resentful feelings towards happy couples and envy towards those admired by others.

Lying on my bed, wrapped in my arms, I wrestled with a different view of me. My mind normally forgot about my unpleasant side. There was a cloud of innocence I often stepped into, where I was a good person and could never feel hate. There were other escapes I had used, like reading or watching a film. But this was the time to be straight with myself.

The pain of shame and guilt burned through me. Eventually my inner storms would settle, and I lay quiet, allowing acceptance to fill in the cracks. My guilt dispersed and compassion rose up. I could see a bigger picture. Those ugly feelings were as much a part of me as the nicer ones. And there was something lovely about my feelings, something raw and real. They were important to my journey in this life.

Over time, the benefits of this dive into myself were clearer. With acceptance came fresh air, a remarkable freedom. No more pretending to others. I didn't have to run from, deny, or ignore those darker feelings as I had in the past. Being all of them, the good, the bad and the awful, was just fine. I sunk deeper into being me and my insides felt stronger.

One evening Katie led a meditation for members. She asked us to link our hearts, as we entered a half hour period of silence. Afterwards she drew me aside. "What is going on between you and Gerd? I saw flames of fire connecting you. I'm kinda shocked. Your flames were smaller, and muted, but his were strong and pure and reached to you powerfully." Surprised by Katie's perceptiveness, I revealed to her all that had transpired between Gerd and I.

Clearly, my heart was connecting to him in a real, apparent to others, way. I struggled with following my rule to keep God first. God and Gerd became blended in my eyes. It was as though our relationship was transparent and God smiled through. I shared with him what Katie had said and my surprise and shock. His response was less than open.

"I am not interested in you in a relationship type of way," he declared, setting up a clear boundary. "And I don't trust Katie's ability to see these things correctly. I haven't told you yet, but I found someone, Katrine, with whom I feel total recognition and a deep spiritual connection."

After hearing what Gerd said, I wondered about the meaning of all of this. His panicked response shook me up a bit, but it didn't hurt. My heart continued to glow towards him, unwavering. My belief in the importance of our relationship never weakened. It was not frivolous; something bigger was pushing me to keep on.

The next day we did not see each other. Was he avoiding me? Would our friendship ever be the same? My relationship with God, however, went deeper and deeper.

I wrote in my diary: *"A dark night it is for me. I step into the blackness, and there is no one to distract me, no goal to focus on, to steer me away from my total dissolution. I move inward and all there is, is God. God warms my heart. God guides my steps. It is a God I cannot see, a God that guides from behind, that surprises me with Its wisdom. I must surrender. Release my control. Have nothing except Self. I stand without supports. I move without inner direction.*

I have blamed others for deserting me, for not being there when I needed them. But I am so deep within, where others cannot go, or even understand to go. So I am alone, angry and disappointed. And yet, in the depths of my aloneness, I feel God's gentle hand. There in the darkness is something lovely. So I move deeper within."

A few days later, our small meditation group met, consisting of Katie, Gerd, Richard and myself. Despite my reservations, it was lovely to see Gerd, and he seemed to feel the same. In meditation, my connection with him was as strong. My heart expanded and my whole being joined with his. Silent tears and great gut sobs filled me, for I knew God was near. Over the years, I strove to put God first in my life. It was clear, in this relationship He was first. God beckoned me forward through my love for Gerd. Our relationship was a spiritual one.

An Experience Week focalizer asked me to do an Inner Life Sharing on Sunday evening. The timing was odd, for that weekend I struggled with some darker emotions and depression. Hoping for relief, a passage about giving our pain to God seemed to help. My mind slipped into a meditative trance as I found my way to the sanctuary. Without any effort on my part, no visualizing, commanding or praying, my pain lifted. Happiness filled me. I felt light as a feather. Recognizing how spirit supports me always brought me joy. It was this I could share with the group that evening. Seeing and accepting our uglier parts was part of the work. Allowing spirit to scrub us clean and remove our burdens was another part. Some of the guests pulled me aside later to talk more about my experiences.

I kept some distance from Gerd since our meditation and my realizations. We exchanged words, but my deeper feelings were blocked. One morning we met at breakfast, and afterwards a sadness rose up. *"I want to be with Gerd."* Then and there, I knew I must open to this man, if for no purpose other than life was better with him. I invited him to meet.

He came to my room, bringing a book he was reading. We spent some time talking about our individual journeys, and then he read to me from *Light on the Path*. Each passage touched me to my core. The wisdom from his reading and his radiant self humbled me. I was nothing, an ignorant student, embarrassed to even be with Gerd. He understood when I shared my reaction. "That is how I feel around Katrine and Richard." It was a deep lesson in humility for me.

That night in my dream I made love to Joshua, a big brawny man I was corresponding with. The next morning, the difference between dream Joshua and Gerd's non-sexual love, was painted in relief. I could only acknowledge that our platonic relationship was my path to God right now. Gerd was my teacher.

FEELING ONE'S FEELINGS

Throughout my journey, the most useful technique for purifying my personality issues was allowing myself to feel my feelings; to let emotions take me along, until I was nothing but a flood of anger, shame or grief. Afterwards, I lay spent on the bed, the silent stillness of my being reflecting the calm after a great storm. From that place, I would stir again, cleansed. Besides having a safe space for allowing myself to feel fully, I also needed a willingness to accept what came.

In my practice, unfelt feelings bore the brunt of the mental health problems I commonly found. A healthy person allowed their feelings to move through and be released, like an occasional rain shower. Hanging onto anger, or holding back grief, tended to clog our system and, over time, moved us to build more complex holding structures. Anxiety or depression resulted, hiding what lay beneath. Usually the trauma occurred early on in a person's life, and made for a miserable midlife. Finding someone with whom one could share past secrets and release pent-up feelings, provided enormous relief and the possibility of a better tomorrow. Acceptance was the most important tool I provided for them, that they could eventually provide for themselves.

21

The Synthesis Workshop

The Benefits of Meditation

*In my dream, a woman asked about my child's father. "Who was
he?"*
"Gerd, of course," I answered.

Assigning a role for certain people to play in your life is too
easy. A 'platonic friendship' sounded fine as a way to describe
Gerd and I. My mind might have made that decision, but the
energies flowing through me were so strong the word platonic
did not do our relationship justice. We can assign different
meanings to our feelings, but I struggled with the intensity of
mine.

"Can I talk to you?" Gerd asked, as he walked into my room.
He had just moved to Drumduan, my home for a few months. I
helped persuade him to make the move. "It's only a five minute
walk from Cluny, and incredibly quiet. And the wooded path to

get there is lovely." So my friend had joined our small group of members living in the house.

It was a day of dark clouds and light rain. I sat at my desk, looking out the window, when he came in. My hand motioned towards the bed. "Have a seat."

"You need to know," he began, "I am not interested in you sexually. I am destined for Katrine."

Not something a woman wants to hear, no matter who was saying it.

"I do know," I said softly, thinking he must need to repeat this message to make his position crystal clear. He had made a similar statement a few weeks earlier.

"I feel you are generating a lot of attachment and desire energy towards me," he continued.

"Oh." My stomach churned, my secret exposed. He was right. Astrologically, we shared a potent conjunction: my Mars was at the same degree as his Venus, usually portending strong sexual attraction and compatibility. Perhaps it was the magnet that kept me drawn to him, despite the rejections he doled out. Moving forward with him, I felt like a sacrificial lamb, destined for slaughter. But truth be told, it was hard to imagine being with him sexually. My draw to him was something different.

"I know that's true at times," I confessed, "but I don't give it credence. My lesson is on how to love as purely as possible, and I don't always get it right. It's my issue."

Gerd always seemed to be managing our relationship better than I. Yet I had not realized how afraid he was of my love.

"Gerd, you never even let me hug you. My touching sends you scuttling back three feet. It is clear we are not destined for something sexual."

I continued. "There's no denying we have a strong connection. What we do with it, I don't know."

My heart sank as I reflected on our situation. It was getting messy.

"All I want is for us to do what's right!" Tears were tucked behind my words. Was I too idealistic, hoping my loving would not threaten our friendship?

"I can see us focalizing workshops together," he offered.

"Yeah," I nodded apathetically, having little desire to do a workshop with him. I was following the trail of breadcrumbs my guidance and my feelings were leading me on. Putting a form around this friendship was not what I needed. How I felt about Gerd had so much more to do with me and my lessons, and less about us.

"Hey, Ian is focalizing a workshop called Synthesis. Richard and I are going to do it. Why don't you take it with us? I'd really like for you and I to do this together."

My spirits lifted. Gerd wanted to do a workshop with me, to stay connected.

"I'll try," I said, feeling inspired again. It was time to drop my intensive inner focus anyway, and step out a bit. This workshop would provide a way to ease myself into a more expanded life.

The workshop was a month long, and I was one of the three members given permission to take it. It focused primarily on spiritual growth, meditation and other practices. Special lecturers joined us, including William Bloom, a British author and educator, and Carolyn Myss, an American medical psychic and author. William spoke of practicing meditation and recognizing levels of psycho-spiritual growth. Carolyn talked about her experiences of the seven chakras and the health issues that accompany each of the seven.

One lesson was especially impactful for me. Carolyn asked us to consider the difference between our wants and our needs. That evening, I listed my desires. None of them were needs. My needs were very simple, and fulfilled. It was my wants that kept me up at night, that created a dull ache of dissatisfaction, and the thought, *"I don't have enough."*

Realizing this provided me some distance, allowing my wants to fade into the background. Those subtle threads of panic that attend me when disappointed were severed. And I settled into the security of knowing my needs were completely taken care of.

Our group divided into two during the workshop, separating Gerd and I. For one week my group stayed on Iona at Traigh Bhan, a house donated to the community years before. I took long walks, often passing the farms that dotted the only roadway. I loved watching the new born lambs leap about, playing with each other. Other times I veered off into the fields to climb to the high point of the island. The wildness of the windy island met a wildness in me that I seldom touched into at Cluny.

One evening a group of us gathered in the sanctuary. Robert, who in his outer life was a Catholic priest, led us in a ceremony to bless the earth.

He then asked me to recite the 23rd Psalm, a favorite of mine.

"The lord is my shepherd, I shall not want…"

It was a powerful moment. The words resonated clearly. The

sacred was in the room. *This must be what a priest feels when they hold mass.* It was a garment I felt comfortable stepping into.

Soon, changes in my relationship with Gerd would bring out less priestly parts of myself.

THE BENEFITS OF MEDITATION

My nose itches. Try as I might to stay settled, I have to scratch it. My eyelids raise and my eyes catch the flicker of a bushtit moving in the plum tree next to my window. I watch for a short time, shifting a bit in my chair to find that sweet spot of comfort, then close my lids again. "I am that I am. ... I am that I am. ..." My body settles slowly and occasional small trills of pleasure ripple through it.

"I need to cut that grape vine." The thought bubbles up over the drumbeat of the repeating mantra. I don't let it take me out of the relaxed, trance-like space I am in.

Over and over, my mind ranges from a deep quiet, to a dream-state where stories unfold, to remembering I am reciting a mantra and fingering beads of my mala. There is a slight pressure in my brain as it maintains the quiet amidst the flurry of available distractions. I make it through the twenty minutes, then my body springs up into action, desiring to get on with the day.

A zen master would be appalled at my lack of discipline and poverty of ritual. Yet I never judge my performance. Meditation and I are old friends. There are times when I go deep, and fill with sparkling energy. And there are restless times, when bothering to set aside a half hour feels too much. Yet I do, for the benefits are great.

Benefits are important if one is to practice meditation regularly. At first, we reap at least two, enough to keep on going. The carrot that dangles before us, motivating our start, is relaxation. It feels good. And relaxing the mind feels really good.

Another benefit comes as we catch ourselves thinking, caught in our reverie. Each time we rein in our thoughts and return to the object we are meditating on, our mind forms a deeper pathway into being. Rather than getting caught in the continuous streaming of thoughts, we become aware of a spaciousness. And that state of spaciousness returns throughout the day, when we are active. Sitting in traffic a moment of presence enters as we notice our whining irritability. Engaging in a discussion with our brother, we become aware of our automatic reactivity and find the time to think before speaking.

Other benefits accrue over the days and years of maintaining a meditation practice. Stress reduces. And positive feelings of love and joy are easier to access.

When I first learned at age nineteen, it was through a method called Transcendental Meditation. Each participant was given a Sanskrit phrase to repeat over and over during the twenty minutes we spent meditating. The repetitions helped to keep our minds focused, less apt to wander around. I have changed my phrasing over the years, using English phrases that were more meaningful to me.

There are other methods. For very physical people, a walking meditation may work better. Some prefer to focus on an object, or on nothing at all. A friend described his experience of bliss while staring into a candle flame. One method I found fascinating was to outline an image with my eyes, focusing on each point along the line. I used a diagram of a labyrinth. My mind slowed til each moment unfolded, bringing ripples of pleasure.

Establishing a habit takes effort. Setting up a consistent time and place, where one is not interrupted, is helpful. And I use my mala as an aide. Similar to counting Hail Mary's with my rosary as a child, moving the beads through my fingers is a soothing ritual for remembering where I am.

Meditation is not prayer; it is the act of quieting the mind and experiencing the self that exists behind the thoughts. So people of all spiritual or nonspiritual persuasions can do it. Quieting the mind is the first step towards connecting with our soul. And that might be the best benefit of all.

22

The Game

Synchronicity and Symbols

I shivered in the early March wind on my way to the beach. A walk was needed, it was clear. My belly felt a pitter-patter, and there was a slight shaking in my limbs. In a few hours, my group from the Synthesis workshop would play the Game, and I had some bouts of dread. Despite it being a game, it was not fun. Despite all the amazing aspects to it: a magical synchronicity, a mirror for oneself, and a microcosm of our life choices; despite all of that, the two times I had played in the past had not been fun.

This would be my third. How many times would I be stuck in one spot, burdened by pain tokens? How many times would I have to reveal some sensitive issue to the group? I could not take more pain, that was clear. Looking out over the North Sea, I bargained with God. "Alright, I'll play the Game if You promise to not bring me any more pain." A ping rippled through my body. *Good to go*, I thought.

"The Game of Transformation" is a board game developed by two members of the community. My first encounter was during Orientation. For the first day of three, we met in small groups to discuss our purposes for playing. The second day we played on a large board, while focused on those purposes. Two guides joined us, taking on the role of God for the game. On the last day we shared with the whole group our experience.

The game moved each player through levels, from the physical to enlightenment. The cards we drew gave us insights and pointed to our inner obstacles on the various levels. The angel cards, which now sell at bookstores around the world, were originally developed for this game. Each angelic quality we drew provided support for the level we were on. All our cards were meant to connect to our purpose, though we might have to look a little deeper or wait a little longer to understand the link.

Perhaps too excited to play, my eagerness moved me very quickly through the levels and I ended up completing much earlier than the others. It may sound like a win, but it was not. I had not allowed the game to unfold its gifts. "Your purpose was too easy," Kathy, one of our guides and one of the original developers of the game, had said.

Fiddling around, I helped as the others continued to play. Growing in my confidence as a helper, at one point I grabbed some blessings to give to another player. Kathy slapped me on the wrist.

"Stop that! You are not God. That is my role. I give out the blessings." Sheepishly, I put the blessings back. I had overstepped into being 'God' before my time.

At the end, Kathy pointed out how my goals limited me.

"You are like a fish that reaches the water's surface only to be scared off by your own reflection. You swim back to the depths to work on more parts of yourself, rather than dare to reach for the sky. You're on the edge of creating, yet too afraid to take the leap." Her feedback rang true.

My second time playing the Game was as a new member of Cluny Garden. In early February, Theresa suggested we grab the chance before spring turned into summer and guests filled our garden group.

Kathy was one of our guides, the same Kathy who led my game during Orientation. When we met together to develop our goals, Esta, a long-term guest in the garden, revealed she had a previous disagreement with Kathy and was nervous to be vulnerable around her.

"If it seems like I am being put in a bad spot, would you support me?" she asked.

"Of course," we all chimed in.

Playing the Game is intense, and one can feel vulnerable. A supportive group makes the experience easier.

An hour in, Esta drew a card. It said: *You are set back by your mistrust on your present level.*

Kathy leaned in. "How is this true for you?"

Esta shifted nervously in her seat, appearing to become more and more uncomfortable. "Uhhh," she mouthed, trying to deflect from Kathy's probing question. She did not want to answer what was apparent to all of us. She mistrusted Kathy. Finally Esta broke from her gaze and called out, "Where are you guys? I thought we had an agreement."

The atmosphere thickened in the silence, and Kathy's voice

sliced through it like a knife, "WHAT! You all conspired behind my back?"

The delicate field we had created was ripped to shreds at that moment. The air sizzled with emotional electricity.

"No, no. We promised to be supportive. That was all," Peggy said. The rest of us nodded. We weren't sure how to actually save Esta from answering Kathy about that card.

Kathy asked us to file out, so she and her co-leader could talk. After a short break, we returned to complete the game although the air still crackled a bit. Ending the game was a relief. I headed straight for the forest, where walking slowly helped remove the stain of that experience.

This third game unfolded with magical precision. We met in the Park Building library in front of a roaring fire. The room was dominated by the round table, set for five players and two guides. I was quiet inside, having surrendered my need for control after my 'walk and talk' by the sea. The game reflected my passivity right back to me. The others were already making moves around the board, while I waited and waited to be born. Beginning to feel left out and frustrated, I wondered, *was the only way to avoid pain to not be born?* Eventually someone's miracle allowed me to incarnate. Someone else's miracle moved me quickly up to the mental level, where the others were, bypassing the physical and emotional ones.

My first insight card read: *Time for a change? It's your chance to be GOD. Intuit now whether the change is appropriate and then toss the coin. If yes, insights all around. If no, all others receive a setback.*

I didn't need to check inside. This was the same issue from my first game, over three years ago, when I wrongly played GOD. Of course it was now my time. After all the work I'd done, it must be my time.

The coin flipped then dropped onto the board. A symbol for a tear was on its surface. NO. I cringed as my fellow players all received a setback card, and pain.

Slapped down after my hubris, the implications flashed before me. It was the negative fallout from my early morning 'deal with the devil.' While I emerged pain free, every other player was brought pain as a result of my actions, a profound lesson. You can't fool the game. You can't fool life. You can't shortchange your own progress. I could not swear off pain anymore than I could cut off my head. It was essential to my growth.

From then on, I would check inside before leaping forward with assumptions. My lesson held me in good stead. Another player gave me an insight card from his Miracle. It reassured me I could trust myself to do it right the next time. *You allow the purposes of the Christ to direct and guide you. SO – create a whole new realm of peace and love.*

What followed was synchronicity at its finest. I landed on a 'make an intuitive decision now' square. This time, after checking within, I knew the left path was the right one for me. Rolling the die, my piece landed on a Miracle, moving all players onto the Love level and creating indeed *a whole new realm* on our microcosmic board.

One can live a life of slow growth and learn thru the pains and pleasures of career and family how to navigate, how to make the best of life, and, for some, how to eventually find a more transcendent understanding. But coming to Findhorn, for me and many others, was an invitation to leap, a willingness for fast-paced lessons. An important tool we were taught by the Game, was to look more deeply into experiences, recognize the symbolic meaning at their core and acknowledge one's part in creating them.

I left behind the Game after this one, feeling complete. It was only much later, when my life was more settled, that I bought the simplified board game and invited my friends to play with me.

SYNCHRONICITY AND SYMBOLS

I cannot explain the mechanics of the synchronous events that commonly occurred at Findhorn. Drawing the perfect angel card, bumping into the person we were just thinking of, or finding a pair of bird wings after wishing for some: it is hard to understand how these events are possible. Some believe our minds search for a compatible explanation, that we rationalize the relevance. Or that the events are coincidences, not a sign of a greater connectivity.

I have read that synchronous events increase in the lives of those on the spiritual path. Is the universe bending to assist us? Is the natural world that pliable? In my view, synchronous events are like messages from the spirit realm. They have meaning for those who recognize them. It is commonly found that if you pay attention to your dreams, you'll have more. Similarly, if one sees meaning in synchronous outer events, they'll experience more of them. The material world is less rigid in their eyes.

One morning on my way to work, years after my time at Findhorn, I was talking to Spirit about my death. I had been thinking whether to invite an earlier death or leave later. But thoughts of my niece and others who needed me, including our planet, were important to consider. In that moment I made my choice. I vowed, a bodhisattva vow of sorts, that I would stay to help. My belly filled with joy and I drove on, aligned with the world around me.

And the world seemed to adapt. The cars moved aside, the lights turned green, as I flowed down the avenue and onto the freeway. I pulled into a grouping of light grey cars, then noticed further in front were eight more light grey cars. In my rear mirror, I saw the same. For about ten minutes, I had the only colored car for hundreds of feet in both directions. Unmatched and traveling at different speeds, this was not a collection destined for a particular place. This was the magic of synchronicity. Its meaning was clear to me. My choice had been blessed.

Seeing beyond the physical appearance to the underlying purposes of some event, object or person is the language of the soul. Our dream life conveys meaning if we look carefully. Our external life has meaning as well. For example, my home is filled with thick oak furniture. The oak is beautiful, yet there is more to its meaning for us. It is strong and solid, enduring over time, a furniture that reflects our need for stability. Automobiles often reflect the driver: swift, loud, tiny or expensive. And when we are in a kerfuffle, our cars can act up, mirroring our confusion.

As a therapist I learned to adapt my observations to my clients' tolerances. Very few gained the distance to look at an event and recognize the lesson in it for them. They were often immersed in their world of relationships, engrossed in their own thoughts, feelings and reactions. Lessons were hard won, sometimes painful, repeated again and again.

I pointed out the meaning of their experience, taking them one or two steps further in their understanding, by linking their present to the past they could not see as relevant. We all need someone at times to point out our blind spots.

But for those who aspire for spiritual growth, recognizing the meaning behind experiences is a welcomed key; asking within for understanding is a way forward. And our world changes as we do.

23

Gerd's Last Gift

Cathartic Healing

During the workshop, Gerd and I often hung out, riding back to Cluny in his little car. But his friendship with Kate, a smiling American, was growing and soon they became lovers. Frozen into place, I watched them together. She now rode in his car. She was the one he took everywhere.

I did what I always do, shut down. What had been a rich friendship was suddenly dead to me. My heart was silent. It was painful to see them drive off, and have to take the bus home. Painful to see them holding hands. Numbing my feelings and getting on with my life seemed my best option. But being that checked out was not possible.

My anger was building. Noisy housecleaning used up some of my energy, as my mind raced with all the reasons I should be pissed, none of them true. *Gerd clearly needed a woman to be with him and used me until someone more appropriate showed up. He deserted me for another. What I offered wasn't good enough.*

Feelings of relief emerged as well. I was freed and grateful to be out of a relationship that made me feel so much and work so hard.

"Why am I angry? Am I jealous?"

It didn't feel like jealousy so much as loss and embarrassment. I was the one left behind. The twisting pain of abandonment triggered a memory of a dream from many years earlier.

In it *I was a young Native American girl, courted by a white man. We married and moved away, leaving my friends and family behind. I explored music on his piano and my knowledge of the world expanded under his tutelage. But when he died, I had to return to the tribe. Returning grated inside me, after criticizing those people and their lives for so long. And here I was, forced to face my negativity and swallow my pride. As a widowed tribe member, the leaders relegated me to a group of widows and grandmothers, who took care of the children and prepared the food. My future would be a life of toil and boredom. There were two choices: stay and make the best of the situation or leave. Eventually I left, choosing aloneness over conformity, danger over mediocrity. My life ended in the forest.*

A similar choice rose up at this crossroads with Gerd. I could leave my life here at Findhorn, after enduring so many friends leaving, such loss, or stay and create a contented life alone.

I stopped spending time with him, and looked to a separate future. But Gerd would not have it. Shortly after we returned to the community from Iona, he came to my room. I didn't want him there. It hurt too much.

He stood in the doorway. "I know something is going on between us because of Kate. Can we talk about it? I don't want to lose you as a friend."

I turned away and paced the floor, anger rising. My answer was packed with all the vehemence my belly could muster. "No! I don't want that." My hands splayed out in front of me as if to push him away. "I don't want you in my life anymore…"

He stood passively, listening while I continued, "You left me. You don't care. You never showed caring or love towards me. You were always impersonal, unfeeling, and I'm done." My petty brutality was apparent, but I let my drama play out.

He stepped forward. "I do care about you. That's why I'm here. Please, don't let this ruin our relationship."

I backed further into the room. "No! You speak in third person and platitudes. Theoretical language. I am human. I have feelings." I batter rammed him with my words.

Gerd took it in, silent yet undeterred. He aimed for my heart, ignoring the argument I tried to brew.

"Bonnie, please."

I stopped moving, and settled into a quiet deadness. From a distance, I saw him grab my hands and look directly into my eyes. "Please don't shut me out." His pleading touched me, my defenses softened.

To respond, I had to look away. "I know my heart is not open to you." My voice choked. Aloneness was better than being left.

Slipping my hands out of his, I let them fall to my side.

A conflict was rising within me and I teared up in frustration. "If I opened my heart to you, it would be to say, 'Fine. Leave me. I'll still love you.' and I can't do that."

"I won't leave you. I'm not leaving you. I wouldn't be here if I was leaving you," he said.

While looking out the window and watching the leaves shuddering in the wind, thoughts milled around my mind. *It's true, he has not left me. He came here. He is enduring my wrath. And he has stayed.*

At that moment I saw the gift. Here was a man willing to fight for me despite my rejecting him, just as I had been willing to love him through his rejections. The scales were balancing.

I sighed, the view through the window receding into the background as my heart opened.

"Thank you," I said softly, under my breath.

I turned back to him. Another sigh. I wiped my eyes.

"Thank you for not giving up on me." I hoped he understood what a gift it was.

Gerd cracked a smile. The energy in the room changed; the storm lifted. We were again old friends, having been through so much together. And yet, I could not see a future for us. Perhaps we did not need much more from each other, having reached this denouement.

We hugged. "I am happy for you and Kate," I said, and meant it.

Gerd left the community soon after. I did not feel abandoned; I felt complete. He went to the US with Kate and I lost his whereabouts. A year later a postcard came from him. Back in Germany, he was living what he called a monastic life. The card pictured a monk in dark robes sitting in a beautiful, sunlit garden with his back hunched forward, his face in his hands. "This is how I feel most days," he wrote. It was then I knew he had chosen aloneness.

CATHARTIC HEALING

Sometimes it takes just one emotional release, one catharsis, to shift things entirely. The waters of emotion purify our being. The negativity that clung so persistently is gone. Strength returns.

I could not have predicted the way forward through my pain. The path to that release is never prescribed. But strong emotions have a way of leading us to where we need to go. And Gerd was the key that unlocked a lifetime of abandonment issues for me. The door opened and the pain left.

24

Met by David

The Ladder

I was at the end of a chapter of my life and my energies were low. How does one stay emotionally invested in the community when those friends invested in leave? Morley, Peggy, Theresa, Allison: all had moved on. And now Gerd had gone. Like the destruction of a Buddhist sand mandala, the small structures of support I had created with my friends dissolved away and I was forced to find comfort within myself. It was a month of dragging feet and half-hearted attempts at living after he left.

As day followed night, so my energies rose again. A few clues spoke of a new direction. First of all, a caravan in the Park became available for me to move into, a sign of how ready I was for more independence. Most of the longer-term members lived in the Park. Making meaningful social connections might be difficult as a newcomer, but the benefits, such as making my own meals and having a home all my own, outweighed the possible hardships.

And the angel card of BIRTH kept appearing. It was the card I received at the end of our spring conference a week before, the card I drew yesterday and the card that lay on the counter at Reception this day. "Looks like a big change is coming for you," Arlene, a member, had said, peering over my shoulder at the picture of an angel holding a baby.

I laughed. "And it's my birthday tomorrow."

Whatever lay in my future, I was not feeling it the next day. It might have been the saddest birthday ever. Usually someone was around I could ask for a hug and birthday greetings from. But not this time. A walk in the forest by myself was the best I could muster.

After a day of misery, I was done with self-pity. No more loneliness. Wonderful people had left the community. But new wonderful people stepped off that bus every week.

The next day, David leaped onto my bus. After work, I waited on the bus to Cluny. Some of the long-term guests were joking with me, when he jumped up the steps. Full of energy, he first smiled at the driver, then scanned the bus til his smile alighted on me.

"Do you mind if I sit here?" he asked.

The bus had plenty of empty seats.

"No, of course not." I scooted over.

David was revisiting the community after many years. He and his previous wife had been members during the 1970's. As we talked, the bus took some sharp turns and we slid around the seat. He exaggerated the centrifugal forces on him, falling into me and then into the aisle. He was like that, full of playful energy. We laughed and crashed into each other.

A few days later, David joined me in the anteroom of the

sanctuary before the 6 pm meditation. We playfully bantered back and forth as we caught up. He was very direct in his gaze and evasive with his words. I tried to ask him questions, wanting facts to add to my knowledge bank. It was not easy to pin him down about his life. He redirected our conversation, time and again. Over the week, I would realize he wanted me to let go of my mental constructs and just be present with him.

He shared his observations about the community. "Most of the people here are dwelling in their higher chakras and not really embodied." I struggled to not take offense, but his words rippled through me. Something to think about later.

The next evening, we rode home together and shared about our day. Both heading for the tea trolley, we decided to walk out to the wall by the greenhouse to talk more. He told me his story, that he had experienced a personality death and realized his body was all he had. His body was his truth finder, his guide. He called it an enlightenment experience, that he had no ties holding him down anymore.

"Wow! I am surprised," I said. Enlightenment was an ideal many of us strove for in our community, though it is likely few understood what it truly was.

"It's not all it's cracked up to be. Too much energy, too much awareness." He said his body guided him here, but so far his experiences have been disturbing. He could not dream, could not meditate and found he evoked negative reactions in people. "What is going on?" he wondered.

After finishing his story, he looked at me, his eyes alive and searching. "Wow! You've just given me an incredible gift. Thank you."

"What gift?" I asked. I would find myself always two steps behind his thought processes.

"Your power," he responded. "Your womanly power."

I blushed, a little uncomfortable. But also felt seen. He had looked into me, perhaps for the first time.

"How frustrating! You've hid it for so long. That must be hard."

I was flying in the dark, yet somehow knew the direction he was going in. "Yeah, it has been."

"You've chosen a really good place to nurture it. Out in the world, other powerful people have caused you to withdraw, because you felt yours wasn't needed. But here, with all these softies, in this cloud of no resistance, you can grow into it." He stared at me, his gaze challenging. "You realize this means you are on the way to leaving."

"Yes, I know." It might take a bit more time, but I was getting stronger, strong enough to hold my own in the outer world.

"I've got it!" he leaped to his feet. "MEET ME OR GET THE FUCK OUT OF MY WAY. That is your mantra."

The power of his words hit me like a monsoon. Dizzy, I grabbed onto the stone wall. Here was someone speaking to my essence. He was spot on, knowing immediately what my life had been like. And for him to say "MEET ME..." I had silently screamed that thought for so long.

Never had I felt so understood.

"Stand up and say it," he commanded.

Embarrassed and laughing and stunned at the rightness of it all, I stood up and repeated the phrase to him.

"Good," he said. "But you can do better. That one came from

your throat. It needs to come from your womb." He placed his fist on my stomach. "This is your source of female power."

Oh my God. For years I've been hiding my power, to not threaten others.

He continued, "To me, your power is very feminine. Not the gentle, fluffy, receptive kind, but strong and very female... I won't ask you to say it again. Better to test the waters first before stepping in fully."

We left the greenhouse. My world was spinning, as if I was on LSD. David had injected so much energy into me, my perceptions were altering. I went for a walk to settle myself down.

Later that evening a dance was held in the ballroom. The room was rather somber until David joined us. At first he played around, doing splits and cartwheels while he danced to the music. Did I mention he was a modern dancer in Boston?

Once warmed up, he began to reach out to others. He managed to engage almost everyone in the room, laughing while he called them out to join him on the dance floor. With the men he played. With the women, he took them in his arms and seduced them in the dance. With those who were shy, he was subdued and respectful. With those willing to be experimental, he experimented. Like the mischievous Tom Bombadil from Lord of the Rings, he worked the room, waking people up and infusing new energy into them.

When it was my turn, we switched back and forth, leading and following. We had so much fun, playfully exaggerating our male and female roles.

As I gathered my things to leave, he whispered in my ear,

"Remember, you can meet someone. There are men who can meet you."

A longing filled my belly. "Well yes, you meet me."

David smiled then softly punched my gut. "You are so powerful!"

It was Saturday morning and I found David waiting in the foyer, luggage packed, preparing to leave. We agreed to write each other.

Then he looked straight at me. "You should be glad I'm leaving."

"Why?" I asked, again two steps behind.

"Because I would never let up until you had a total personality disintegration."

I believed him. "Yeah, I guess I'm not ready for you yet. Perhaps in a few years."

As we hugged goodbye, he thrust his pelvis close to mine. "You know, I can't help but relate to you in a sexual way. Your energy just invokes this response in me. You are a warrior woman."

David's leaving was sad, but also a relief. He was intense. And he held up a mirror, forcing me to face my feminine power. It would take time to integrate that view. I feared most men felt my power was too much. It was nice to know some would relish it.

Shortly after David left, I moved into Matchbox. A little aquamarine-colored caravan nestled in a block of pine trees in the Pineridge area of the Park. Behind the trees were sand dunes covered in gorse bushes and heather. The North Sea lay beyond.

I could slip out behind my caravan and find my way to the sea whenever I wished.

My first act was to light up the peat stove, then explore the place. Matchbox's living room had raw wood paneling and sculpted wood shelves. One of the many members who had lived there previously was obviously a wood smith. The place was small, with a tiny bedroom and bath. But I loved fitting into tight places. My baths involved bent knees, a far cry from the huge tubs in Cluny that could fit two very tall people easily.

Living in the Park, there was more time in the evenings. I often rushed to the sea after work. Walking the shoreline, thoughts about my day came up. And then the wind, the waves and the vast horizon would remind me to step into the present. If the forests of Cluny helped me to listen within, the North Sea purified so much in me that needed cleansing.

THE LADDER

David met me, and I met him. We shared a similar spirit of playfulness and daring and power. He saw further into who I was, at that point, than I knew myself. Further than I knew was possible. But I don't believe I offered him much. I was the receiver rather than the giver. He seemed a few rungs higher on the advancing ladder to the Spiritual.

Where ever we are on that ladder, we give or we are given to. We hold out our hand for those slightly below us and reach for the hand that comes from slightly above us. We cannot rush, for each new rung requires lessons to be learned, lessons to be integrated into our being.

Findhorn was a great spot for meeting people near me on the ladder, for it drew seekers from across the globe. One's personal teachers could be found in such a center, such as Gerd was for me. But learning never ends and we move on, finding new teachers and new students.

The Earth is often depicted as a school house, providing experiences for a wide range of people, from the very young to very old souls. We shape our lessons by choosing our directions. I imagine little magnets within that pull us towards those people and experiences that help our next step. And though the ladder is just a simplified image of what occurs, it helped me to understand my relationship with others in our community.

25

Beyond the Veil

Traversing the Unseen World

Spending the summer in the Park was lovely. The days were long. The sun dipped below the horizon for a few hours, only to rise again. The birds sang day and night. At Cluny I had pulled the shades to sleep. At the Park, I let the light in. Nature was so close there.

On a Tuesday morning in July, I walked to the sanctuary from my caravan in Pineridge. Usually half asleep, today felt different. I was alert, my mind clear. The breezes, the sparkling drops of dew and the bird songs sent ripples of pleasure in me. There was a spring in my step; my senses were heightened.

Perhaps it was because of my letter to Tanya last week: apologizing, suggesting we could find a way to be together, telling her of my love. Her response arrived yesterday. She was excited. After she worked out some things with her family, she would come. I felt like skipping on that dusty path.

The last time Tanya visited the community, I had been

overwhelmed by my own life, focused purely on getting through, one day at a time. Having a visitor was one stressor too many. She found her own way, by joining the Departmental Guest Week and visiting with friends.

On her last day we met and walked into a beech grove near Cluny. The canopy filtered light onto a path leading to a small bridge. Our legs dangled over the water as we talked. It was good to spend time with her. I walked her to the bus, and watched as she rode off, on her way to the train station in Forres.

A letter came a few months later. She was in the Philippines, having joined Doctors without Borders to help people with little access to medical care. Done with Germany, she was unwilling to stay there longer. Tanya had begun her own walkabout.

This day felt eons away from those days. She was back in Hamburg. And I was ready to be with her. Happiness bubbled up inside me. Perhaps she'll live here. Perhaps we'll settle in the States. So many possibilities.

The sanctuary had a few early meditators already there. Entering a quiet state this morning was easy. I seemed to be plugged into an energy socket, sprits of joy sparking through me.

At the noon meditation, a love, pure and powerful, entered me. It's strength shook my chest area, then spread through my whole body.

My friend, Katie, stopped to chat afterwards. "What is happening?" she asked. "Your eyes are glowing. It's hard to look at you."

"I don't know. Maybe it's cause Tanya's coming. There is so much love going through me I can barely stand still."

The thought of Tanya continued to be with me over the next three days. I talked to her when alone, almost believing her there. Every night, her arms wrapped around my body as I slept. Every day love filled my being. *Tanya must be thinking of me too,* was my explanation.

Walking back to my caravan from lunch on Thursday, questions about our future together crossed my mind. Was I limiting my life by staying with Tanya, when there was so much still to learn about being with men?

I dared to ask, *"Tanya, could we be together in a looser sort of way, so I could date men as well?"*

An image of us living in a white cottage, supporting each other's lives, appeared alongside a resounding *"yes"* from her. The impossible seemed possible in that field of unconditional love.

On Friday, those pure feelings of love disappeared. My morning meditation was normal again. That afternoon, while writing letters in response to questions about the community, a phone call came through. It was from Tanya's sister. *She must be calling to tell me when Tanya will arrive,* I thought. It would explain her presence in my thinking for the last three days.

But her sister's story was a different one. Tanya had fallen from a horse and hit her head. She was rushed to the hospital and was in the operating room for hours.

"She didn't make it," she said.

My ears heard the words but I didn't quite understand. "What did you say?" Slowly my mind grasped her meaning. "She didn't make it?" My voice shook as I asked, "She died?" A fuzz clouded my senses. Distantly, I heard her tell me Tanya's funeral date.

"Do you plan on attending? Would you like us to send you some photos?"

I tried to focus on her questions. "No, no." Photos seemed meaningless at the moment. And could I attend a service without crumpling up? Arrange transport to Germany? Function enough right then to give her my address? It all seemed impossible.

Feelings began to flood my thinking and I couldn't stay much longer on the phone. I managed to ask, "When did she die?"

Her sister responded, "Early Tuesday morning."

Hanging up, I turned to Ann, who was watching me with questions in her eyes.

"My friend died." My blank stare covered the tidal wave of panic beginning to wash over me.

"I've got to get out of here!"

Ann told me later she was unaware of my history with Tanya, and did not understand my reaction. At that moment, I didn't care. I ran outside, not sure where to go. I needed to crawl into a hole and let myself be taken over by that tidal wave threatening to consume me.

I stopped at the office where Katie worked. She looked up, suspending her greeting after seeing my face.

"Katie, Tanya's dead!" My cry filled the room.

She stood, but I didn't want her response. Spinning around, I left, shutting the door to her office, shutting out anyone attempting to enter my field of view. Hurrying to my caravan, I closed myself inside and let the waves take me.

The pain! It tore at my insides. I had lost her, she was gone.

How much she had given me, how much she had taught me… of surrender, of love. *Her short life must have had purpose*

187

for her. She was restless, lived lightly, unattached to her career. She was searching for something more. Perhaps she had no more reason to stay here on Earth, I thought.

My mind shifted back and forth between two levels, one very personal, absorbed in the pain of my loss, and the other more universal, where Tanya floated out in the starry blackness of space, enjoying her freedom.

At one point, my friend, Katharina, knocked outside the door. I didn't answer, didn't want to hear her say, "I left some food on your step." How could I eat?

Saturday, Christa came to my door, letting me know there would be a service for Tanya, to be held at the Nature sanctuary on Sunday. News of her death had spread through the community, unknown to me. My pain was still raw, but I forced myself to attend. The circular sanctuary was filled with people. She had made such an impact, unknown to me. Carol, the psychic who gave me a reading while still a guest, led the service. She had gotten to know Tanya fairly well over the years. She read a poem Tanya had written that spring in one of Carol's workshop, and offered me a copy. In it she wrote of beginnings and endings, living and dying. It seemed the tethers to her life were thinning even then.

In certain Buddhist texts a period of three days between one's death and one's soul moving on is described. After the three days she spent with me, I felt her no more. But because of her visit, never again would I doubt humans survive death, for she had given me proof.

TRAVERSING THE UNSEEN WORLD

A year after John and I married, we toured Europe on a belated honeymoon. We visited friends at Findhorn and my brother in southern France. But the time we spent in Paris held a particular magic for me, and a mystery. We toured art museums, ate amazing food and visited Notre Dame.

The queue for the cathedral was long and we advanced slowly towards the entrance. Just as we crossed the threshold, an intense energy field surrounded me, like I had entered a deep sea of pressure. The field overtook my senses and tears streamed down my cheeks, unbidden, uncontrollable. I grasped for John's arm. "Something weird is happening to me. I am being overloaded with feelings, and can't stop crying. I need to sit."

John guided me to a wooden pew, where I felt my way to the seat. Then he left to explore the place. My hands shook as I held onto the wood. "What's going on? Is this the millions of people who have been here? Is this the millions of souls attached to this place?" No other cathedral had felt this way. I had no answers, but did know my tears were not from pain or sadness, just the intensity of it all. Ten minutes later, John returned.

"You'll have to help me. I'm shaking and can't see past my tears." I clung to his arm for support as he walked me around the interior. We merged with the crowd and moved towards the exit. No one else seemed to be having my reaction. The feeling never diminished, the tears never stopped, until we crossed the threshold into the bright day. Gone. The feelings were gone. "Oh, I am so glad to be out of there." I wiped the streaks off my cheeks.

The cathedral has a history of hundreds of suicides. Perhaps this is what I felt, the impress of ghosts upon the building. Or had I been connected with Notre Dame sometime in my past? It remains a mystery to this day.

Being visited by a recently deceased person is not uncommon. There are many stories of loved ones visiting people. Besides Tanya, one other being visited me, my dog Gennie. When she passed over, I mourned her loss for weeks and wasn't moving on from my grief. Perhaps someone from above took pity on me, for one evening as I lay in bed, Gennie leapt up and joined me. We cuddled until I fell asleep. She was not in physical form, but I knew it was her none-the-less.

It was a gift, her letting me hold her for such a long time. An anxiety-prone rescue dog, she avoided cuddling when alive, as she avoided all entrapments.

Afterwards, I was able to let my grief go.

Otherworldly experiences are rare for me, each one a carefully orchestrated lesson in what is possible. I was trained to question, to be a skeptic, which created subtle restraints upon my beliefs. Exploring the paranormal was a mental interest in my earlier years, but never a confirmed reality. Only an actual experience could completely convince me. These few incidents, scattered through my life, offered me a certainty of the transcendent, magical world we live in.

26

The Spiral of Growth

The Spiral of Growth

You are standing before a portal of initiation. The way forward is through fear of failure or fear of the potential within. From a personal reading by David Cousins.

I danced with fear, taking two steps forward, then pulling one step back, a pattern scrolled upon the map of my life. Each time greater responsibility was given to me, at a certain point I crumbled, retreating til ready to get back out there. At times, others were disappointed. Mostly strength was built, a long road to strength.

The only way to escape fear was to face it. When hid, fear's ominous chain wrapped me in its grip. And the grinding spectre of failure haunted me deep within. I would have disappointed myself if defeat won. Sooner or later, the challenge had to be faced. And after, confidence filled me. It would have been nice to say my confidence was permanent. But I couldn't. New fears always emerged. And again I would fall back, then collect a head of steam to force my way through.

Was it just treading water, my repeating the same reactions time and again, getting nowhere? This was not how I saw it. Even when immersed in a new challenge, my growth and my expanded capacities were apparent. The image of a spiral, moving upward, described the pattern. Each loop took me a little higher, and each dip did not go so low.

Potential is a 'hairy beast', for one can feel its urgings, but finding the way to fulfilling ones potential is not always guaranteed. We all have our own ideas of what fulfillment means; some aim for fortune, notoriety or children. The thought of a loving relationship was my idea of fulfillment. But that was not the path I seemed to be following. The bars of my potential's prison were made of fear, and empowerment my only antidote.

During the reading from Carol four years earlier, she mentioned my power. *It feels like you have learned the lesson of power previously. Now it is about bringing it into connection with joyfulness and sensitivity; bringing a delicacy of touch and lightness to it. It's connected with leadership and especially with helping others.*

My chances for leadership in the community increased slowly, first by focalizing Cluny Garden and then by leading groups in the Guest Department. I tried to hold the threads of leadership lightly, yet my attachment to making each guest's experience a good one became a problem. A nervous breakdown shredded that attachment and woke up a rage that sent me spiraling out of the community.

Joining the Communications Department upon my return was a welcome breather from leadership, not challenging at all.

The highlight of my job was a gathering of Resource People (RPs) in early summertime.

The gathering was easy. The RPs did not need the guidance an Experience Week group would. They led Findhorn-style groups in their own countries and visited the community often. The week was more of a celebration than a duty. We arranged sacred dance, art, trips to the beach and hikes into the Cairngorm Mountains. Ann and I shared about the present community, catching them up with the changes to this living, breathing entity called the Findhorn Foundation. And they shared their world with us.

I came alive that week, reconnecting with my love for running groups. There was something about holding the space for others that called to me. Personnel was looking for a focalizer to lead the new Orientation program. Rather than a discreet, time-limited group, the program would run continuously, with orientees coming in and others leaving at the end of each month. Each person would stay in the program for three months and then transition into membership. I applied and was accepted for the job.

The new program kicked off in the fall. While working in the Guest Department my second year as a member, I discovered the position of workshop leader was isolating. An image reoccurred that illustrated this: *I saw myself standing on a mountain top, assisting those in my group to climb up. I waved to focalizers on other mountain tops, but could not bridge the gap.* This time I was prepared for the isolation a group focalizer experiences.

None the less, holding the program together took its toll on me. In the third month, the flu hit me hard. Underlying the external symptoms was an exhaustion of nerves. The orientees fended for themselves for a few weeks as I recovered.

Upon returning, strong and happy to be back, I opened up a discussion about my absence. "I apologize for being gone. Not a great thing to happen in your orientation program. So, please, this is the time to share how it was for you."

Most members kept it simple. "No problem."

One member, Vera, saw it differently. "Well, I'm not happy. It was disappointing that you were unavailable, and there was no backup group leader I could talk to." Her anger was apparent.

She was right, of course. Yet she grabbed the opportunity to point out other problems she was seeing in our group. Her energy was intense and I suggested we meet in private to talk about it. She refused.

A few days later, as I walked past her at lunchtime, she called me over and asked for a favor. After a moment's thought, I said, "No, I don't think so."

My answer surprised me. She was surprised as well. "Why not?"

"I am not going to go out of my way to do something for you after you lambasted me in front of the group last week, and did not want to talk about it later. You can't expect me to forget what happened so easily."

A shocked look spread across her face. I had come back at her with the same force she had sent out to me.

I watched myself speak with a well-modulated power, aware of the lesson in it for her at the same time defending my rights.

"You can't put out such anger and not expect it to return," I continued, knowing that angry energy does not just dissipate. It enters the people it is directed towards, foments inside, and has consequences.

Vera was silent, and I left feeling judicious, not angry. She had taken a shot and I, in return, took a shot. We were even.

Later that day I reached out, to try to heal the rift we had created.

"Vera, I know we have a problem and I wanted to talk about it. Would you be willing to meet with me?"

Her eyes opened wide, like a deer in the headlights. Clearly she did not want to be anywhere near me. Having her anger returned to her was not what she was used to, especially by a focalizer, and she did not feel safe. She said no.

I tried again, softening my voice and lowering to my knees. "I'm not angry and I don't want to hurt you... Please... I only want to heal what has happened between us."

Finally, she agreed.

We met in the small meeting room on the second floor. She sat far away, arms crossed in front of her. I was gentle, holding out my hand, as if entreating a wary deer to come forward. Eventually her body softened and she leaned in, willing to share her side. I stayed undefended, taking in her feedback and appreciating her perspective. We left the room as friends.

When Vera graduated from Orientation, she gave me a bottle of essential oils she had blended using a pendulum to select the right combination. The scent was deliciously thick, a musky rose fragrance. It included blue rose oil, the most expensive oil she had in her collection, she told me. I was honored.

My fall into stress got back to Personnel. Although handling everything thrown my way by that point, they determined I needed a co-focalizer. "No thanks" was my response, but they insisted, so beginning in March, Maria joined me.

Maria, a wife and mother, had no experience leading groups. And she had never gone through Orientation. She married a member so became a member by default. Personnel had no one else available, and she was eager to work.

Maria was a lovely, sensitive woman with a delicate demeanor that belied her steely strength. Although she would eventually become a very good focalizer, in the beginning, her lack of group experience was more of a detriment. Her personal sharings were glaringly uninspired. She described a day of shopping, or challenges with her children. She did not know how to share her deeper, more vulnerable self. It was important to me she set an example for the orientees, so I prodded her for change. At times I found myself with an extra student rather than extra help.

And she struggled with me. Overly convinced about certain aspects of the program, I was a tough taskmaster. She fought to be heard, for her vision to be implemented. Over the months we worked together, we both changed. My stance softened and she stepped up.

A few months in, a dream foreshadowed my future. *I knelt by a sparkling stream, drawn to the flickering lights that flowed past. From its depths a clear quartz crystal, one of the mineral kingdom's highest expressions, rose above the surface. It was a gift from the greater realms.*

As I held it to the light, Maria knelt beside me. She desired it. The crystal was given to me, but it was only a material representation of something greater. I did not need to keep it. Knowing Spirit had honored me was enough. So I offered it to her.

Soon I would pass on the focalization to Maria. My time at the community was drawing to a close.

THE SPIRAL OF GROWTH

Every lesson moves us forward, deepens our connection with ourselves, even if it seems as though we are standing still. In my later years as a psychotherapist, I often had to reassure my clients who watched themselves repeating a similar pattern of bad habits. "Rather than a full circle, it's more like a spiral. Your path may loop down, dipping into familiar situations again and again. Yet inside you're different. You've grown in awareness, strength and self-acceptance. For each loop, you respond a little differently; your path circles a little higher."

During my years at Findhorn, I returned to my previous patterns of fear and withdrawal, time and again. Yet, inside a solidness was forming. A surprising passion emerged as I expressed my self, a stronger self forged from the crucible of my fears.

27

Thy Will and My Will are One

The Mystery School That Is Findhorn

It was June, 1989. Maria and I, as focalizers of the Orientation program, had enrolled our group in a Psychosynthesis workshop. The Institute in London sends a practitioner up to Findhorn only once or twice a year, so we could not pass up this opportunity.

Personally cautious about taking part in another workshop, I learned digging into myself can be exhausting and any revelation requires a time of integration. Workshops are offered every week in the community. To avoid overload, it is best to enroll only after questioning within: *Do I have the energy for it? Can I handle one more insight?* There was no choice with this one, however. As focalizers, we were expected to participate.

Actually, the timing was right. A question had been growing in me for weeks, and needed an answer. *Should I leave? Is this the right time for me to go?* A restlessness stirred inside. I floated above the activities of simple living and missed the small struggles that a regular life holds. Most of my needs were handled: my meals were made, my bills were paid.. As well, many of my friends had already left the community. The outside offered more enduring relationships. The option of leaving shined brightly.

On the other hand, this workshop would be the start of a training program offered by the Psychosynthesis Institute at the community, so interested members could become certified practitioners. Moving on would cause me to miss this opportunity.

We met downstairs, in the family room at Cluny. The summery day showing through the window was tempting; the room was dark in comparison.

The workshop began, as many have done, with clarifying our purposes. My purpose was simple: an answer to *Is it the right time to leave?*

The Purpose Exercise was followed by a guided imagery session, where we visualized walking into a house and meeting the people there. They represented various parts of ourselves, called sub-personalities. My imagery journey began in a meadow: *In front of me is a two-storied house. Overgrown plants cover the exterior. Inside, the walls are bright white, the home neat and well cared for. The living room is carpeted, the beige couch cushions overstuffed. A man greets me, dressed in a business suit. He is polite, cool and very rational. It is immediately clear he is a conforming, responsible person.*

Going up the stairs, a woman's warm smile welcomes me. She has long rippling hair and wears a delicate, gauzy gown. Her room is ornate, with painted screens, large fans, palm plants, and colorful scarves hanging from the rafters. An easel rests near the window and paintings are strewn about. She lets me know she does not want to go downstairs. She is happy being here.

I move on, venturing into the basement. It is cool and dark, with a smell of dank concrete. In the corner is a shriveled little girl, crippled and in dark rags. She is angry and feels trapped. There is a willful rebelliousness about her. She needs to be accepted, to be loved, yet I don't want to. Her willfulness is of no use in this world. The man upstairs is the one who keeps her in the basement.

Out in the meadow, I invite the little girl to join me. She hobbles out. I can see how much she needs her freedom, but cannot imagine how she will make it in the world. She needs to grow more. Perhaps she will find her way. Perhaps the woman upstairs can help her.

As we emerged from the imagery, we are asked to choose a sub-personality to focus on. The man, the responsible one, seemed to hold the key to the house of myself. Immediately my sinuses swelled up. The phrase *I am here to support others* floated by, a phrase that informed much of my time at Findhorn. "Whew," I sighed. "What a demand to put on myself." Shades of my mother's influence, ordering me about, her eldest daughter, as she entertained her friends. But more importantly I could see my own hand in maintaining this mantra. It has been lifelong in the making. The burden pressed down on my shoulders.

The man and the woman were brought together in my imagination. I posed my question, *"Do I leave the community? Or not?"* The woman said *"yes"* and her qualities filled me. *I am light and free to be creative and follow my own way. Looking to the man next, he said "no."* Pressure again alighted on my shoulders. *I am dutiful, hard-working, and responsible.*

It was clear they needed each other. The woman had no

way to ground her expressions and the man couldn't access inspiration. We were asked to draw a symbol of the chosen sub-personalities working together. The image of a vase holding flowers came to me.

Next, *the little girl came forward. She spoke out, "I have to express myself. I am a creator. Help me show myself. Love me. This world is malleable. I can change it to suit me."* My responsible, conforming male reacted. *"I keep you down because you don't fit in this world. Your willfulness is about creating rather than adapting."* My father's voice sifted through my awareness. *"No one wants you to mess up the system. Join an institution, like Findhorn, then you won't be tempted to be willful."* Somehow, somewhere, sometime these two parts of me would need to work together, if I was to be unified and whole. For now, she would be allowed to grow.

Coming out of my trance-like state, the implications were overwhelming. There was a lot to think about, later. For it was break time and I yearned for a breath of fresh air after that exercise. Upstairs I went for a snack and a cup of tea, then out the side door to watch the garden grow. The day was calm and sunny. Butterflies fluttered on the breeze and the bees alighted on bobbing flower stalks. Whew! a much needed respite.

After the break, Margo, the leader, guided us in a pre-birth meditation to connect with a wiser part of ourselves that can see our purposes for incarnating. My wise being told me: *You will be coming to Earth with many gifts that won't find easy expression. You need to experience a series of wombs, so that deeper parts of yourself can be born. You mustn't push, but allow those births their own timing.*

Being raised by my parents, moving to Findhorn, my

friendship with Gerd: each was a womb preparing me. My parents taught me how to fit into the normal world. My home at Findhorn allowed my spiritual self to expand and gain credence. Being empowered by the community to speak out, to show myself, helped me lay aside many of my insecurities. And loving Gerd opened my heart fully to the pain of earthly relationships. I allowed another to touch me deeply and will always be grateful for that.

One of our final exercises was about will. Roberto Assagioli, the creator of Psychosynthesis, believed the will, and ways for handling power, were important aspects of psychological growth.

The leader led us in the three steps of a reflective meditation exercise. We first purged our mind of the simple ideas and associations on the topic of will by writing down as many as we could: ...William ...free will ...will power ...etc.

Then she shifted us to a deeper view of will. What is the purpose of this quality, what did it look like to express it in our lives, what images do we associate with it? My experience of will at this point was a feeling of solid power in my belly. It was the key to creating the life I choose. Having the willingness to surrender to a greater good was also important, I learned a year earlier.

For the final step, once our minds were cleared of the mental noise, we entered the quiet... blending with the quality of will in meditation. It was at this point that a repeating mantra began to drum inside me.

...*Thy Will Is My Will*

... *My Will Is Thy Will... ...*

Over and over the verse echoed.

202

…Thy Will Is My Will… My Will Is Thy Will

The phrasing changed in different ways. Sometimes I was speaking to Spirit, sometimes I was Spirit speaking to me. We blended as one in the rhythmic refrain.

An image came up: *I am kneeling in front of a radiant Being on a throne. In awe, I lower my head. The Being rises, lifts a sword and taps my right and then my left shoulder with the blade. "Go forth and live your life," the Being says. "Fear not doing harm, for our wills are one."*

Tears flowed quietly down my face. A knowing was forged inside me: my will and Spirit's will are one. It was clear for the first time.

The meaning of this experience unfolded over the next days. So afraid of harming others, I did not live myself fully. My power, my strength, my truth-telling and my spiritual knowing were judged as too much by my father and remained largely unnoticed by my mother. I feared others would feel the same. Deep in my core, I was not okay. It made me weak, ineffective and unable to face the challenges of living.

But now, after five years of inner work, my fears were assuaged. Expressing myself was perfectly aligned with what is right. Because I will always wish the best for others, my power could stay intact as I stepped out into the world. I was complete.

It was time to leave, so over the next month, I began to let go. Many evenings after work, I raced to the North Sea, letting the strong winds blow against me. Here, my previous experiences had rewinded; the joys, the love, and the pain a part of the lessons I learned. Here my tears had been swept away, my face to the world scrubbed clean. Being at the sea helped me be 'in the moment' more than any other place.

And when at Cluny, my old vegetable garden drew me, the garden that was mine no more. Another focalizer, another expression. All good. The woods of Cluny Hill reminded me of the months of feeling my way into the darkness.

When meditating in the Park Sanctuary, memories of Tanya's spirit visiting me and those cries of pain that followed were laid to rest.

During our last attunement, I released the mantle of Orientation to Maria, and gave her a quartz crystal.

Leaving, I carried much less emotional baggage than I had brought. My insides were strong; my inner resources more accessible. Ready to leap into a new life at thirty-eight, I felt reborn. Packed and waiting for the bus, no one lingered, hoping I would stay. The time was right.

THE MYSTERY SCHOOL THAT IS FINDHORN

Alice Bailey wrote in Letters On Occult Meditation *about future mystery schools. Her book, said to be dictated by a master who dwelt in Tibet, was written in 1922. The location and qualities of future schools of esoteric studies were described. Preparatory schools would be located near larger cities, for accessibility. As well they would be built near expanses of water, a reminder for the student of the purification needed to advance. It was predicted that one of the preparatory schools would be located in Scotland or Wales.*

I read this only after being at Findhorn a few years. It was not talked about freely in the community. What did it matter anyway that

Findhorn might be one of these schools? The point was to get on with living and learning.

With so many varied purposes for visiting and moving to the community, we all may define the place differently. For me, I lived at a mystery school. I said yes to my soul directing the journey. I was given the experiences that moved me on, step by step. And I willingly faced my demons.

I left the community purified, cleansed of my past emotional woundings, cleansed of many of my limiting doubts. After Findhorn, my inner light shone through me more easily. Yet it would take more turns of the spiral, more challenges, to get me to today and open the way for tomorrow.

28

A Soul-Infused Personality

Moments of Soul Connection

We enter our lives with what seems to be a blank slate. Choices guide our steps forward. And suddenly, as we look back over the decades, a pattern emerges. Our purposes are revealed. Our selves have been structured, embellished and settled into a wholeness that was impossible to predict in our earlier years. Our souls find expression easier through this integration.

What is a soul-infused personality? That question lingered in my thoughts for many years after my time at Findhorn, when Dorothy Maclean had used the term. She experienced her soul ever present, and had no need to meditate. To forever ride on the crest of the soul sounded wonderful. Yet it was only in my latter years I could grasp an inkling of what that felt like.

My soul came through me more easily as a child, catching butterflies and ecstatically leaning into flower cups. When the light rays of God's world shined through the clouds, gratitude filled my chest. But that innocence became sheathed in defenses by my early twenties. More and more, the feeling of disconnection from my source led to unhappiness, although spiritual texts reassured me I was never truly separate. Re-finding that 'easy' access to my soul proved a distant hope, … did not seem easy at all. The path was clouded and disjointed, distractions inviting me to stray. Yet looking back now, I see my direction clearly. My emotional wounds needed to be healed and the pain released. Thoughts about my capabilities needed rewriting. All in all, a transformation needed to happen.

In my twenties, reading about another's search for a spiritual teacher inspired my own seeking. Yet I never found the teacher for me. And perhaps having one was not meant to be my way. Finding healing and spiritual growth within a community setting, with no actual teacher, was unexpected. In that supportive environment, I learned from my interactions with those around me. Rather than an external teacher, my internal guide led me. Rather than controlling for safety, as the ego is apt to do, I leapt in.

Five years later, I left, knowing my spiritual source lay within, had always lain within, a constant companion. Nirvana may not have been achieved, but my psyche had been cleansed and prepared so my soul could express through me more easily.

Joining my mother and sister in the bustling capitol of California, Sacramento, was a challenge. The sun in August burned bright and blisteringly hot compared to the grey skies and cool breezes of Scotland. All the moisture was sucked out of my pale skin. Outbreaks of poison oak threatened to take me down, as my body adapted to the Sacramento Valley area.

When meditating, my being immediately shot up, feeling

floaty and ungrounded. I stopped my practice for a few months, to adjust myself to the less refined level of my new life.

After five years of vegetables and grains, I returned to eating meat. My whining about the absence of vegetarian dishes at restaurants had become stale. Having an enjoyable dinner with my family was way more important than imposing my vegetarian identity onto our gatherings. And my body seemed to prefer meat.

My heart, that I had worked so hard to open, had to be shuttered in this more invulnerable world. Strangers tended to misinterpret my friendliness as flirting or just too much. Being snarled at more than once was not pleasant.

Sharing my Findhorn experiences in a relatable way took many more years. For my first step, I enrolled in a spiritually-oriented Master's level counseling program in San Francisco. My time at Findhorn would serve me well in a counseling career, a dream since college. After completing my master's, a job opened up for work as a counselor at Northlake, a large group home for the mentally ill. This had its purposes. Before beginning an internship and then setting up a private practice, it felt important to become acquainted with the most difficult cases, to understand the lengths the human mind could go. Diving into the deep end was a way to manage my fears.

Northlake became a proving ground for my heart. I found myself bending and blending in response to the people there. My overactive brain had to take a back seat when we talked. Many of the schizophrenics at my job only became confused when questioned, as if they were being grilled under a bright light. My perceptiveness had to mute and my heart to open, creating a soft space for us to relate in.

One afternoon, Mica, a resident there, approached me. "Can I talk to you?"

Stopping mid-track, I smiled. "Sure."

He was in his twenties, slim with dark, shoulder length hair. He wore sloppy blue jeans and a black t-shirt, pretty much the same type of clothing I was wearing.

Shifting nervously from foot to foot, Mica stumbled through his words. "Well I'm a little afraid to say this, but ... I wanted to tell you ... I ... ah... I love you."

Everything stopped in me.

"Yeah, although I don't want to freak you out. More like friends. You work hard here and try to keep Northlake clean, which I appreciate. You've been helpful to me and really listen when I need to talk. And I see how much you care for the others."

"Oh wow, that is so nice." It was a carefully worded response, positive yet vague.

He looked down as if to find his words, "You are a real person, original. I've never met a professional like you before. ... Actually, I don't feel towards you like a friend; it's more like one human loving another human."

He paused again, then pleaded, "Please don't change towards me because of what I said."

I stood quietly, respectfully. His courageous admission awed me. Warmth filled my heart. "No, no, I won't."

Mica continued complimenting me, beginning to perseverate. And one can only take so much, before tuning out.

I raised my hand. "It's okay. I get it."

He backed up a bit, frightened by my response.

"I don't want you to change because of what I said. Are you

okay with me telling you this?" He looked at me questioningly, like a little boy. His liquid brown eyes showed his vulnerability, as if his fate rested in my answer.

"Oh, totally. Thank you so much. I'm glad you shared that. It's such a nice thing for you to say." Silently, looking into his eyes, my soft fist tapped my heart a few times.

Mica's love did not faze me, did not trigger fear of his attachment. Viewing love impersonally was already a lesson I had learned. Mica knew this, unconsciously perhaps. For me, every appreciation was part of a world of love shared by all of us.

My heart opened easily at Northlake. Each person showed themselves without guile. Some mornings, residents surrounded me, drawn to the love I felt for them, the love we shared. Opening my heart to those in need became a major component later in my counseling work. My purpose, decided upon so many years ago, was being fulfilled.

Sometimes other sides of my emerging self came out unexpectedly, and were less pleasant. Ray, a school mate of mine, was talking about his struggles with his boyfriend when a higher energy filled me, and I spoke, helpless to stop myself. *"You are hiding in these distractions. Who you are is so much larger than what you spend your time thinking about."* My soul had called his soul out.

Afterwards, I quickly backtracked, shocked by the knowing that had come through me. "Oh my God, I am so sorry. That was uncalled for."

"It's alright. You don't have to apologize."

None the less, my apologies kept coming. I was ashamed of revealing that part of me, of putting my friend in that position, of being so out of control. What was happening to me? Those breakthrough moments occurred a few times over the first years after my return to the States.

There was truly nothing to be ashamed of. It was the birthing pains of my awakening soul, seeking expression in the world. Yet speaking from my soul while engaged in more mundane conversations was embarrassingly out of place. Fortunately, after every clunky attempt at bringing forth those energies, I was reminded of the mantra: "My will and thy will are one." Even if fumbling, my motives aimed for good.

Over the years, sharing my inspirations are more in my control. And my timing skills have hopefully improved.

Sometimes the energies unveiling in me were powerful. One afternoon, after a troubling interaction with a friend of mine, a fire began to burn inside. Later that evening, I wrote:

"I feel like a beacon of fire tonight. I can't seem to sleep; can't drift away from the powerful heat and light pulsating through me. I told a difficult truth to a friend, and may lose her.

Should I have waited until calmer; softened the intensity inside? Yet the light sent was not meant to be hurtful, it was meant to wake her up. Over the years, I've learned to be careful with my words; to let my intense feelings inform the message rather than be the message. Sometimes we have to be holders of the light, sometimes senders of love. Today I hold a beacon of fire.

Light is only one aspect of my inner flame. Passion for truth, passion for transformation, these are the purposes that lay behind the lighting of my beacon. When someone has blockages, at times I am called to set it free, mix it up and see where the pieces fall. I don't often feel this intense drive for change. But when it comes, it is a powerful swell of my heart, and I don't settle easily. That is how I feel tonight, powerful and unsettled.

I'm wondering, will she consider me too bold, have no right to my perception? Will she wake? Change? Have I lost her? Only time will show me how the pieces will re-assemble. There are no guarantees. That is the danger and exquisite joy of being a beacon of fire.

Fears slowed the pace of establishing myself in this new life. The five years spent in the community did not eliminate my tendency towards social anxiety. My struggles continued, likely would always continue. But it was clear, facing my fears was the only way forward. And I wanted to move forward. Often friends gave me the much needed nudges.

After what felt like eons of celibacy, I tried dating, getting a chance to hone my instincts with men. At one point, ready to give up, Katie from Findhorn chimed in. "Don't ever give up. Not even if you fail a thousand times, try, try again." And so I did. When the time was right, my future husband came into my life.

Applying for an internship took some time. Could I bear the growing pains and pressures of establishing a professional role? This time Loren, the American who danced on the kitchen tables at Cluny, pushed me forward. "You gotta do it. You can't miss your chance. How will you feel if you don't try?"

A psychic told me the third part of my life would be my happiest. Certainly, retiring from work opened a floodgate of possibilities I was eager to explore. Yet, my soul gave me strict instructions. *Pull away from the outer world. Work in your garden. Release any shoulds you have about helping others.*

Letting go took time. Calming my nervous system, and settling down my thinking, was my job now. Silence and simplicity became my touchstones. I spent many years fiddling in my garden, learning its lessons and loving the small moments, while the country moved further away from a healthy relationship with nature. My happy focus on gardening might just play a small part in creating a more hopeful future, I told myself.

In the beginning my garden looked more like a wild creature to tame. A vision of lush, vibrant beds of vegetables drove me forward. Every time I stepped into my backyard, I stepped into a 'work suit', determined and pressured. My mind was not relaxing. And my heart stayed buried under layers of frustration when my garden's productivity was less than planned, season after season.

The successes in the garden were counterbalanced by failures. For the longest time, I ignored the importance of the soil. Images of fat tomatoes, thick peppers and sweet winter squashes drove me on, while my ground was slowly drained of its life and nutrients. How like me to lust for luscious productivity, while ignoring all that it took to get there. Letting go of my deep desire for beautiful fruit and shifting to a deep desire for life-filled soil took some time. Eventually the fruit became an afterthought, a gift for efforts well spent digging in nutrients.

Caring for the roots of my plants was a reminder to keep my own roots deep in the soil of Spirit. When caught in a web of over-activity, my energies would fail, my insides emptied. Meditating helped reestablish my balance.

Now, my garden nourishes me spiritually, as well as physically. Every time I walk through the beds, its beauty invites me to step out of my thought world. I become gloriously present to the pleasures of each moment. And grateful thoughts have become live wires linking directly to my heart.

Breakthroughs of bliss have increased, occurring spontaneously. One afternoon while standing on a step ladder washing our large living room window, a rush of love filled my chest. Moving the cleaning rags across the glass brought me ripples of joy. I looked around, shining my heart's warmth on the bushes, the hummingbirds, and the breezes of the day. It seems the veil between the material and spiritual gets thinner all the time. And I am always reminded to stay open, David Earl's first words so long ago as he welcomed me to Findhorn.

MOMENTS OF SOUL CONNECTION

A useful, if imperfect, way to picture the interaction between the body, personality and soul is the image of the horse-drawn carriage. The rider sets the destination, the driver directs the horses forward, and the horses move the carriage. If the horses are ill, drug-addled, or simply untrained, they will not be able to work as a team and draw the carriage to its destination. If the driver is a drunk, depressed, or easily distracted, the carriage will be pulled along a bumpy, meandering road that perhaps leads nowhere. The best blending of soul, personality and body is when all our parts work together; when the rider, the driver and the horses have direct communication and alignment of intent.

Looking back on my earlier days, my soul's role seemed to be as a guiding hand, occasionally stepping in when I veered too far off the path or felt too alone. Many experiences stirred my soul but the more powerful moments were few and far between: a bed of flowers, a statuette, a man at a door, a dream image, a choice. Like small gems scattered along the way, they inspired me to keep going forward. I yearned for more, but could not recreate those moments. My soul decided the timing. And searching in the outer world, by reading spiritual texts or seeking special people, was helpful, but did not lead to a connection with my soul.

I have learned, over the years, that looking within is the only way forward, though the direction seems backwards. By talking to my soul, rejoicing in its support, the relationship between us is kept alive. And occasionally a magical spring pours out of me in response to someone or thing. A whoosh of joyful energy, a powerful feeling of rightness, or a radiant love, as if my heart was a sun. These breakthroughs remind me I am not alone here on this planet, that my soul has my back. And distinctions between my soul and personality have lessened, because those blissful moments are also me, the fullness of me.

Acknowledgements

So many thanks to give out.

First, thanks to my critique group, who kept me on my toes, pointing out what didn't work and loving what did.

Thanks to Leila Zalocar for being my muse, inspiring me to keep going and giving me your feedback.

Many thanks to Suzanne Streater. I so appreciate you for reading my book and showering me with your positive feedback.

And I want to thank my pit crew, as David Spangler calls them, the unseen beings who helped me work through my blockages, who prodded me to keep going, and filled me with inspiration. Especially I want to thank Anthony, for reminding me that my experiences will be important to some, and I should push on. We all have our part to play.

Thanks to Tatiana Vila for her beautiful cover art. (viladesign.net)

Thanks to my Findhorn friends. You helped keep the spirit fresh in me.

Finally, my family. John, Bu, and Maya, you are the lights in my life.

ABOUT THE AUTHOR

I attended the California Institute of Integral Studies in San Francisco for my Master's in Counseling Psychology. I worked as a Marriage and Family Therapist for twenty years before retiring. Presently, I live with my husband and spend my time writing as well as teaching classes in gardening. Feel free to contact me at *beaublue4@gmail.com.*

www.ingramcontent.com/pod-product-compliance
Lightning Source LLC
Chambersburg PA
CBHW020447130626
46549CB00001B/334